COMPLEAT FEMALE STAGE BEAUTY

BY JEFFREY HATCHER

★

★

DRAMATISTS
PLAY SERVICE
INC.

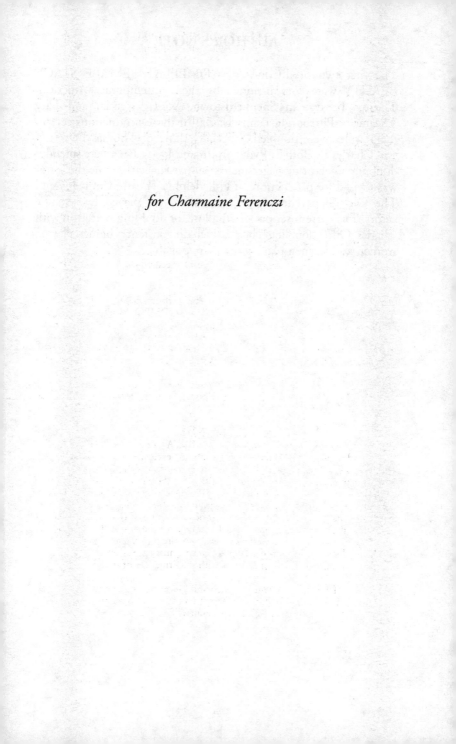

for Charmaine Ferenczi

AUTHOR'S NOTE

The first two productions of COMPLEAT FEMALE STAGE BEAUTY were commissioned by the Contemporary American Theater Festival in Shepherdstown, West Virginia, and City Theater in Pittsburgh, Pennsylvania. In those productions certain major roles were doubled, especially those of Thomas Betterton and Charles II. Both T. Ryder Smith and Doug Rees were splendid doubling as actor manager/merrie monarch. By the time the script was revised for productions at Philadelphia Theatre Company and The Old Globe, however, those roles were played by separate actors. The current script doesn't allow for doubling Betterton with Charles. Other doubling schemes, including instances of men playing women and women playing men, are possible.

COMPLEAT FEMALE STAGE BEAUTY was commissioned by Contemporary American Theater Festival (CATF), West Virginia, and City Theatre Company, Pittsburgh.

It was produced by the Contemporary American Theater Festival in Shepherdstown, West Virginia, opening on July 9, 1999. It was directed by Ed Herendeen; the set design was by Michael J. Dempsey; the costume design was by Moe Schell; the lighting design was by Michael Angelo Tortora; the sound design was by Kevin Lloyd; the hair and makeup design were by Fred Hawck; the stage manager was Kathryn Loftin; the assistant stage manager was Alison Wolocko; the fight captain was Paul Sparks; the casting was by Beverly D. Marable; and the vocal consultant was Sarah Felder. The cast was as follows:

EDWARD KYNASTON .... Dallas Roberts
THOMAS BETTERTON / CHARLES II .... T. Ryder Smith
SAMUEL PEPYS / HYDE /
WATCHMAN / OLLY .... Michael Goodwin
VILLIARS / RUFFIAN .... Lee Sellars
MARIA .... Brandy Burre
LADY MERESVALE .... Melinda Wade
MISS FRAYNE .... Cherene Snow
SIR CHARLES SEDLEY / MISTRESS REVELS .... Paul Sparks
MARGARET HUGHES .... Susan Knight
NELL GWYNN .... Michelle Federer
OMNES .... Members of the 1999 Intern and Apprentice Program

COMPLEAT FEMALE STAGE BEAUTY was produced by the City Theatre Company in Philadelphia, Pennsylvania, opening on October 22, 1999. It was directed by Marc Masterson; the set and props design were by Tony Ferrieri; the costume design was by Lorraine Venberg; the lighting design was by Andrew David Ostrowski; the sound design was by Elizabeth Atkinson; the dramaturge was Carlyn Aquiline; the stage manager was Patti Kelly; period movement was by Elisabeth Orion; the voice and dialect coach was Don Wadsworth; and wigs were by Elsen Associates, Inc. The cast was as follows:

EDWARD KYNASTON .... David Hornsby
THOMAS BETTERTON / CHARLES II .... Douglas Rees
SAMUEL PEPYS / HYDE .... Don Wadsworth
VILLIARS / RUFFIAN / DRUNK .... Michael Tisdale
MARIA / RUFFIAN .... Robin Rundquist
LADY MERESVALE / EMELIA TWO /
SIR PETER LELLY .... Kellee Van Aken
MISS FRAYNE / EMELIA ONE /
THUG / BOUNCER .... Brian Czarniecki
SIR CHARLES SEDLEY /
MISTRESS REVELS / RUFFIAN .... Doug Mertz
MARGARET HUGHES .... Laurie Klatscher
NELL GWYNN .... Michelle Federer

COMPLEAT FEMALE STAGE BEAUTY was produced by The Philadelphia Theatre Company at Plays and Players Theatre in Philadelphia, Pennsylvania, opening on October 25, 2000. It was directed by Walter Bobbie; the set design was by John Lee Beatty; the costume design was by Catherine Zuber; the lighting design was by Peter Kaczorowski; the sound design was by Elaine Tague; and the hair design was by David Brian Brown. The cast was as follows:

EDWARD KYNASTON	Brandon Demery
THOMAS BETTERTON	Steven Skybell
SAMUEL PEPYS / MISTRESS REVELS	Stephen DeRosa
VILLIARS	Glenn Howerton
MARIA	Lauren Ward
LADY MERESVALE	Laura Knight
MISS FRAYNE	Brea Bea
SIR CHARLES SEDLEY	Tom Nelis
MARGARET HUGHES	Jenny Bacon
CHARLES II	Robert Stanton
NELL GWYNN	Marcy Harriell
MALE EMELIA	John Zak
RUFFIAN / THUG	Leo Hiederriter
RUFFIAN / BOUNCER / OLLY	Mark Buettler

COMPLEAT FEMALE STAGE BEAUTY was produced by the Old Globe Theatre in San Diego, California, opening on March 31, 2002. It was directed by Mark Lamos; the set design was by Michael Yeargan; the costume design was by Jess Goldstein; the lighting design was by York Kennedy; the sound design was by Paul Peterson; original music was by Michael Roth; the dramaturg was Scott Horstein; the fight director was Steve Rankin; the voice and dialect coach was Jan Gist; and the stage managers were D. Adams and Joel Rosen. The cast was as follows:

EDWARD KYNASTON	Robert Petkoff
THOMAS BETTERTON	Jonathan Fried
SAMUEL PEPYS	David Cromwell
VILLIARS	Quentin Mare
MARIA	Laura Heisler
LADY MERESVALE	Ryan Dunn
MISS FRAYNE	Christine Marie Brown
SIR CHARLES SEDLEY	Steve Hendrickson
MARGARET HUGHES	Krista Hoeppner
CHARLES II	Tom Hewitt
NELL GWYNN	Kwana Martinez
HYDE	David McCann
MALE EMILIA	Antoine Knoppers
RUFFIAN	Brian Ibsen
RUFFIAN / THUG / COURTIER / SIR THOMAS KILLIGREW	Lucas Caleb Rooney
SIR PETER LELLY	David McCann
MRS. ELIZABETH BARRY / COURTIER	Deb Heinig
MISTRESS REVELS	Ryan Dunn
COURTIER	D'Vorah Bailey

CHARACTERS

EDWARD KYNASTON, 25–30. The last male actor to play female roles in the Restoration.

THOMAS BETTERTON, 30. A major actor of the Restoration.

SAMUEL PEPYS, 40. The famed diarist.

VILLIARS, DUKE OF BUCKINGHAM, 35. A prominent aristocrat.

MARIA, 23. A seamstress.

LADY MERESVALE, 25. A rich fan.

MISS FRAYNE, 25. A rich fan.

SIR CHARLES SEDLEY, 39. A rich writer.

MARGARET HUGHES, 25. The first actress.

CHARLES II, 32. The King.

NELL GWYNN, 15. His mistress.

HYDE, 50. The Prime Minister.

MALE EMILIA, 25. An actor.

FEMALE EMILIA, 25. An actress.

RUFFIAN ONE
RUFFIAN TWO
RUFFIAN THREE
SIR PETER LELLY
THOMAS KILLIGREW
MRS. ELIZABETH BARRY
BOUNCER
MISTRESS REVELS
DRUNK
THUG

PLACE

London.

TIME

1660s.

COMPLEAT FEMALE STAGE BEAUTY

ACT ONE

Prologue

A painted drop of Restoration London. Three knocks of the cane. Lights up on Samuel Pepys. Pepys stands in front of the drop in a pool of light. He holds his diary and looks out front.

PEPYS. "December 8, 1661. To the theater this afternoon to see a play. It is *The Moor of Venice*, from Shakespeare and quite a show of splendour and glitter it is after eighteen years of Puritan gruel. Six months into his restoration and King Charles has made good his promise to bring light back to London, and this "Moor," though black as jealous bile, is brilliantine. Betterton is all one could hope for as the brooding general, but better than even Betterton is his Desdemona. Such eyes, such hair, such lips, and voice to stir, be one Venecian or anthropophagi. The player is Kynaston. And surely he is the most beautiful woman in the house!" *(A loud explosion of stage thunder. Lights out on Pepys. He exits as the drop rises to reveal:)*

End of Prologue

Scene 1

Onstage at the Duke's Theater. A raked stage. A large bed with flowing curtains. No other furniture. A figure lies on the bed. Blonde hair. Flowing light blue robes. Another rumble of thunder. An actor (Thomas Betterton), dressed and in dark make-up as Othello, moves to the bed and parts the curtains. Thunder again. Very loud. Ned Kynaston, made up as Desdemona, starts and sits up.

KYNASTON. "Who's there? Othello?"

BETTERTON. "Ay, Desdemona."

KYNASTON. "Will you come to bed, my lord?"

BETTERTON. "Have you pray'd tonight, Desdemona?"

KYNASTON. "Ay, my lord."

BETTERTON.
  "If you bethink yourself of any crime
    Unreconciled as yet to heaven and grace,
    Solicit for it straight."

KYNASTON. "Alas, my lord, what may you mean by that?"

BETTERTON.
  "Well, do it, and be brief; I will walk by:
    I would not kill thy unprepared spirit;
    No; heaven forfend! I would not kill thy soul."

(Thunder! Kynaston rises and backs away from Betterton.)

KYNASTON. "Talk you of killing?"

BETTERTON. "Ay, I do."

KYNASTON. "Then heaven have mercy on me."

BETTERTON. "Think on thy sins."

KYNASTON. "They are loves I bear to you."

BETTERTON. "Ay, and for that thou diest!"

KYNASTON. "That death's unnatural that kills for loving!"

BETTERTON. "Peace and be still!'

KYNASTON. "I will so. What's the matter?"

BETTERTON.
  "That handkerchief which I so loved and gave thee
    Thou gavest to Cassio."

KYNASTON.
  "No, by my life and soul!
    Send for the man and ask him."
BETTERTON.
  "His mouth is stopped.
    Honest Iago hath ta'en order for 't."
(Rumble of thunder as lights ebb up to reveal side stage boxes filled with fashionable theatergoers.)
KYNASTON. "O, my fear interprets! What he is dead?"
BETTERTON.
  "Had all his hairs been lives, my great revenge
    Had stomach for them all."
KYNASTON. "Alas, he is betray'd, and I undone!"
BETTERTON. "Out, strumpet! Weep'st thou for him to my face?"
KYNASTON. "O, banish me, my lord, but kill me not!"
BETTERTON. "Down, strumpet!"
KYNASTON. "Kill me to-morrow; let me live tonight!"
BETTERTON. "Nay, if you strive, —"
KYNASTON. "But half an hour!"
BETTERTON. "Being done, there is no pause."
KYNASTON. "But while I say one prayer!"
BETTERTON. "It is too late." *(Wild thunder during what follows next: Betterton thrusts Kynaston on the bed and "smothers" him with the red pillow. Knock, off.)*
EMILIA. *(Off.)* "My lord, my lord! What ho! My lord, my lord!"
BETTERTON. *(Still smothering.)*
  "What noise is this? Not dead? Not quite yet dead?
    I that am cruel am yet merciful;
    I would not have thee linger in thy pain:
    So, so."
(A male actor, dressed as Emilia, enters.)
EMILIA ACTOR. My lord, what noise — !
AUDIENCE MALE. Boo!
EMILIA ACTOR. — what, what noise, my —
AUDIENCE MALE. Boo! Boo-boo! Bring back the girl!
BETTERTON. "What, how should she be murdered — "
AUDIENCE FEMALE. Yes, bring back the girl, bring back Desdemona!
AUDIENCE MALE. Bring back Kynaston!
BETTERTON. ... er ... ay, Emilia ... Thou, thou —
AUDIENCE. *(Ad-libs.)* Yes! Hell with the Moor! Give us Kynaston!

Kynaston! KYNASTON! KYNASTON! KYNASTON! *(Betterton tries to struggle on. But it's no use. He fumes. He sighs. He turns and looks at the bed. As the chants of "Kynaston!" go on, he marches to the bed, pulls the curtain open, and yanks Kynaston to a standing position. The audience cheers on as Betterton moves aside and gives Kynaston center stage. Kynaston curtsies. Then he bows and removes his wig. More cheers. Finally he stops the cheers.)*

KYNASTON. Please ... We still have one more scene. *(Audience laughs as Kynaston dons the wig again and flops back down on the bed. Kynaston rises up more time as if he's forgotten to mention something, but Betterton quickly puts the pillow over his face and presses.)*

Scene 2

The green room. Backstage at the Duke's Theater. Kynaston and Betterton enter from the scene we've just witnessed.

KYNASTON. Damn!

BETTERTON. What?

KYNASTON. It's not working!

BETTERTON. *(Disbelief.)* What do you mean, "not working"? I'm trying to get through to the end and they're shouting "Kynaston! Kynaston!" Haven't even FINISHED the show in three fucking weeks!

KYNASTON. I'm talking about my death scene. It's not quite right. *(Betterton plops into a chair and starts to remove his dark make-up. Pepys enters with his diary. Villiars, Duke of Buckingham, enters behind him.)*

PEPYS. Good show, Mr. K.!

VILLIARS. Brava, Kynaston!

BETTERTON. *(Grumpy.)* You see? THEY like it!

PEPYS. *(Ever eager.)* See what?

BETTERTON. Mr. Kynaston is complaining about his death scene.

KYNASTON. Something is eluding me. Perhaps it's a gesture, a tone ... Tommy, do the lines.

BETTERTON. *(Groans, exasperated.)* Oh, come on, can't I just take off my bootblack and go to a whorehouse?

KYNASTON. Come on, this is important. *(Desdemona voice.)* "Alas, he is betrayed and I undone!"

14

BETTERTON. *(Bored, by rote.)* "Out, strumpet! Weep'st thou for him to my face?"

KYNASTON. "O, banish me, my lord, but kill me not!"

BETTERTON. "Down, strumpet!"

KYNASTON. "Kill me to-morrow; let me live tonight!"

BETTERTON. "Nay, if you strive — "

KYNASTON. "But half an hour!"

BETTERTON. "Being done, there is no pause."

KYNASTON. "But while I say one prayer!"

BETTERTON. "It is too late!" Smother, smother, smother.

KYNASTON. Hmmm.

PEPYS. Maybe if you had a speech.

KYNASTON. WHILE I'm being smothered?

BETTERTON. *(Mocking; like a bad actor.)* "Oh, I am being smothered! Othello is smothering me! Oh, please, Othello stop your smothering!"

KYNASTON. See, that's the thing. There's no time. The dialogue is so "bang-bang-bang!" You know what I think? I think the first fellow who did this role had a speech there and Richard Burbage complained he was being upstaged, so Shakespeare cut it. That's it, Tommy, I'm dying too soon.

BETTERTON. There's an actor for you. "My death scene doesn't go on long enough!" Well, you'll have plenty of chances to get it right.

PEPYS. Yes, grasp the fact, Mr. K., the performance is a grand triumph! *(Kynaston sits at his make-up table, removing make-up. The pillow is set on the table.)*

BETTERTON. This is what I don't grasp. King comes to the play last week —

PEPYS. *(Jotting.)* This is *Othello*?

BETTERTON. This is *Othello* — and he says, King says, "Bravo, Betterton, good show, thrills and chills, see it again Saturday next. Question, though: Could it be a bit … cheerier?" "Cheerier?' say I. "Yes" says Charlie, "something more jolly." And I say, all bowed and unctuous, "Would His Majesty prefer a comedy?" And he says, "Oh, no, *Othello* again, by all means, but make it jolly. " And I say, "Well, Your Majesty, Mr. Shakespeare does end his play with Desdemona strangled, Emilia stabbed, Iago arrested, and Othello disemboweling himself. Do you suggest we do away with that?" And he says, "Heavens no, kill 'em all, just make it jollier." What is one to do with such criticism?

PEPYS. Does Desdemona have to die? You could re-write it so that after Othello smothers Desdemona and Iago confesses, Desdemona comes back to life.

KYNASTON. *(Mock groan.)* I start to groan. "Oh — Oh — Oh-thello ... "

BETTERTON. *(Othello voice.)* "What? Desdemona not dead?"

KYNASTON. "Not quite." *(Betterton cradles Kynaston in his arms.)*

BETTERTON. "I did not mean to smother you. Forgive me?"

KYNASTON. "Oh, all right, give us a kiss!" *(Betterton and Kynaston break from their embrace. Kynaston removes his wig.)*

BETTERTON. Have to figure something before the King comes back; we play *Othello* again day after tomorrow. *(Sighs.)* Maybe we'll get lucky.

KYNASTON. Maybe there'll be an interregnum.

PEPYS. *(Picks up pen.)* Ooh!

KYNASTON. Don't write that down, Pepys.

VILLIARS. What none of you glean is that in his preferences, the King is expressing a particularly salient stage view.

BETTERTON. And what is that, your grace?

VILLIARS. He wants surprises. He's been away —and the theaters have been closed — for eighteen years. Now he's back and the theaters are open, what does he find? The same old things. Poetry, he approves; ideas, he approves; love, death, tragedy, comedy, yes! But SURPRISE him!

KYNASTON. What about sex?

VILLIARS. Mr. Kynaston?

KYNASTON. Vis-à-vis the stage. You claim the King approves love, the idea, but what about sex, the expression?

PEPYS. Poetry can express sex.

KYNASTON. And so can sex. "Fit the action to the word, the word to the action."

VILLIARS. Mr. Kynaston, if you insist on something more graphic, show a tit, the King won't complain.

KYNASTON. *(Looks down his bust.)* And how would you suggest I do that?

VILLIARS. *(Deadpan.)* Surprise me. *(Maria, a backstage seamstress, enters with a letter.)*

MARIA. Mr. Kynaston? A letter for you. *(Smells letter.)* Nice perfume. Shall I open it?

KYNASTON. *(Takes it.)* In front of these ruffians? It may be an invitation to an assignation.

BETTERTON. Lady TitBum perhaps. Or the Countess ChewMeUp.

16

MARIA. You're unspeakably vulgar, Mr. Betterton. How that slop bucket can speak such poetry I do not know. *(Taps letter.)* The letter probably came from one of the ladies. *(Kynaston opens the letter and reads. Villiars tries to peek over Kynaston's shoulder at the letter; Kynaston senses his presence and slaps him away with the envelope. Villiars smiles and backs off again.)*

BETTERTON. What ladies?

MARIA. Upper class ones. Two of 'em. They want to come backstage and be received by Mr. Kynaston. *(Kynaston has now read the letter and put it back in the envelope.)*

KYNASTON. *(Indicates letter.)* Then the letter's not from them. The writing style's too coherent to have come from ladies of the upper class. Two minutes, then bring 'em back.

PEPYS. Why two minutes?

KYNASTON. *(Putting wig back on.)* Got to put my visage back on. They want the illusion, not some Green Room hermaphrodite. THIS, Tommy, is why I deserve a share.

BETTERTON. *(Buries head in hands.)* Oh, no.

PEPYS. What are you two talking about?

BETTERTON. Mr. Kynaston's contract is up and he's putting the screws to me.

KYNASTON. All I want is what is fair.

BETTERTON. You have the best deal in London. Five pounds a week, thirty-two weeks a year, choice of roles, and I provide the handkerchiefs. You won't get that over at Mr. Killigrew's theater.

KYNASTON. I want a share. You make me a shareholder, I won't argue salary, I won't argue clothes, I won't even insist you wash the pillow you shove in my nose! Tommy, I'm as much a draw as you! More so!

BETTERTON. Prove it.

KYNASTON. *(Holds up letter.)* Where's your love note? Where're your ladies?

BETTERTON. A share in the company is out of the question. Tell you what. As a gesture of good faith, as proof that I am seeking to find a way, from this day forth you have approval over the casting of any co-star that takes place upon my stage.

KYNASTON. *(To others.)* You are my witnesses. *(Maria exits.)*

PEPYS. *(Snaps diary shut, stands.)* Noted! And I'm off to another show!

BETTERTON. What, to Killigrew's Theater? The competition?

KYNASTON. *(Mock anger.)* Traitor.

17

PEPYS. Killigrew says he's got some new twist.

VILLIARS. I'll give you a lift. I have to dine at Chesterfield's.

KYNASTON. *(Doesn't look up.)* This evening?

VILLIARS. For an hour or so. *(Turns to Betterton.)* Good show, Mr. Betterton. *(Bows to Kynaston.)* Lovely as always, Mr. K.

KYNASTON. Thank you, Your Grace.

PEPYS. Bravo, Betterton. Mr. K.

KYNASTON/BETTERTON. Pepys. *(Villiars and Pepys exit as Maria enters.)*

MARIA. Lady Meresvale and Miss Frayne.

KYNASTON. *(Rises.)* Entre. *(Two decorously gowned giggling girls enter. Maria exits.)*

MISS FRAYNE. SHH! No! You start!

LADY MERESVALE. I can't — You do it!

MISS FRAYNE. You do it! I'll die!

LADY MERESVALE. SHH! Oh — ! *(Turns, curtsies.)* Mr. Kynaston?

KYNASTON. *(Bows.)* Ladies, do you know Mr. Betterton?

MISS FRAYNE. Are you an actor, too?

BETTERTON. *(Stiffens.)* I played the Moor.

MISS FRAYNE. You look different.

BETTERTON. *(Deadpan.)* Yes, I'm not really black.

LADY MERESVALE. Mr. Kynaston, my friend and I saw the performance this afternoon, we're such fans, I can't tell you.

MISS FRAYNE. She's seen you six times.

LADY MERESVALE. Stop it!

MISS FRAYNE. She has.

LADY MERESVALE. I am a great fan, and I was wondering, well — would you be willing to take a stroll with us through St. James'. It would be such an honor to have you.

LADY MERESVALE/MISS FRAYNE. Please, please, please!

KYNASTON. Well, if you give me half an hour to remove my face and clothes —

MISS FRAYNE/LADY MERESVALE. Oh, no! Don't! PLEASE!

LADY MERESVALE. Mr. Kynaston, we'd like you to leave your appearance "as is."

KYNASTON. *(After a beat.)* Well, then: To the carriage!

LADY MERESVALE. He said yes!

MISS FRAYNE. This is so good! *(The giggling ladies sweep Kynaston off.)*

BETTERTON. *(Sighs.)* Should've left the boot black on. *(Betterton exits.)*

Scene 3

The park. Kynaston and the ladies stroll through the lush green. The ladies fan themselves and giggle incessantly.

LADY MERESVALE. Have I told you how many times I've seen you?

KYNASTON. Tell me again.

MISS FRAYNE. Six.

LADY MERESVALE. Seven today.

KYNASTON. And all of them Desdemona?

LADY MERESVALE. No, not all. Juliet and Ophelia and the one without hands and Lady Mac —

KYNASTON. Don't say it.

LADY MERESVALE. What?

KYNASTON. That name.

LADY MERESVALE. What, Mac —

KYNASTON. Don't say it. Just call them "The Scots."

LADY MERESVALE. Why?

KYNASTON. Because they're Scottish

LADY MERESVALE/MISS FRAYNE. Ahhhh. *(Miss Frayne elbows Lady Meresvale.)*

LADY MERESVALE. *(Whisper.)* What?

MISS FRAYNE. *(Whisper.)* Go on.

LADY MERESVALE. *(Whisper.)* No!

MISS FRAYNE. *(Whisper.)* Ask her!

LADY MERESVALE. *(Whisper.)* Quiet!

KYNASTON. What are you two hissing about?

LADY MERESVALE. *(Turns to Kynaston.)* Well —

MISS FRAYNE. You see — Lady Meresvale was wondering —

LADY MERESVALE. We BOTH were.

MISS FRAYNE. Yes, both of us were rather wondering if you were really, well, a gentleman.

KYNASTON. *(Very dignified.)* Ladies, you have no need to fear for your honor.

MISS FRAYNE. *(Overlaps below.)* No, that's not —

LADY MERESVALE *(Overlaps above.)* We didn't mean —

19

KYNASTON. *(Grins.)* I know what you meant.

LADY MERESVALE. *(After a beat.)* … Well? … Are you?

MISS FRAYNE. *(Pert and annoying.)* My father's a wig-maker, and he says you're a fake! He says you must be a woman.

KYNASTON. Lady Meresvale, what does YOUR father say?

LADY MERESVALE. MY father's in the colonies. But my mother's good friend, the Earl of Lauderdale, says if you're a man you don't have a gentleman's thing. He says you're like those Italian singers, the whatzits —

MISS FRAYNE. Castrati.

LADY MERESVALE. The Earl says they cut off your castrati, then you become a woman.

KYNASTON. I take it the Earl of Lauderdale is not a surgeon.

LADY MERESVALE. *(Stupid but proud.)* No, he's an Earl.

KYNASTON. Well, assure both your father the wigger and your mother's special friend that I am indeed a man.

LADY MERESVALE. They said you'd say that.

MISS FRAYNE. They said we'd have to get proof.

KYNASTON. Proof for what?

MISS FRAYNE. For our wager.

LADY MERESVALE. We made a bet.

KYNASTON. I'm not lifting my skirts.

MISS FRAYNE. Oh, come on!

LADY MERESVALE. Please!

KYNASTON. They've only your word to go on. Say I let you see it and there it was, a big, bulging orb and scepter of a thingy.

MISS FRAYNE. That won't do! We need to touch it!

LADY MERESVALE. NOW!

KYNASTON. Why?

LADY MERESVALE. Because they're watching us. From Courtould Palace. *(They all look up and out.)*

KYNASTON. Your father and your mother's lover want to see you stick your heads under my costume and feel me up?

MISS FRAYNE. Give you a shilling. *(A whistle off. They turn. A dandy enters. A dandy of the first order. He wears a pink and blue doublet, cream cape and cream hat with purple plumage, yellow gloves and brandishes a huge gold stick with a red silk tassel on the head. He seems drunk.)*

DANDY. Women, beware! *(Advancing.)* I see three fish eager and awaiting. Come skewer on me pole!

LADIES. OHH!

DANDY. I know a playful bunch when I see 'em! Painted ladies in the middle of the park, universal sign for "Whores to Let." How much for the each of you?

LADY MERESVALE. *(Seethes, to Kynaston.)* For honor's sake, assert yourself!

KYNASTON. *(Playing a woman.)* My dear, how can I? I'm but a wilting girl!

DANDY. C'mon, now, how much for a fuck?

LADY MERESVALE. DO something!

KYNASTON. *(Sighs.)* Very well. *(Points at girls.)* That one's a shilling, that one's a pence, and I'm five pounds a week.

LADY MERESVALE/MISS FRAYNE. OHH! YOU — !

LADY MERESVALE. Sir! Do you know who I am? I am Lady Aurelia Meresvale!

KYNASTON. She's the shilling. *(Lady Meresvale starts to hit Kynaston. Miss Frayne joins in.)*

LADY MERESVALE. You dreadful horrid man!

MISS FRAYNE. Horrid! Dreadful!

DANDY. *(Digs in pockets.)* Here now, hang on, I've got a shilling … *(The dandy advances. The ladies scream and rush off. The dandy stares after it. He turns to Kynaston who starts to exit.)* Wait-o! Not done haggling yet. *(The dandy blocks Kynaston's way.)*

KYNASTON. I warn you, sir: I doubt you'll find in me what you're looking for.

DANDY. I'll be the one to decide that. C'mon, open up! *(Dandy grabs under Kynaston's skirt. Kynaston sighs. Dandy freezes.)*

KYNASTON. Found a guardian at the gate, did you? *(Dandy jumps back.)*

DANDY. Five pounds indeed!

KYNASTON. Twas the weight, not the price.

DANDY. *(Tears off his glove.)* I shall never wear that glove again! Mark me, bum boy, I shall see to you and re-balance our books!

KYNASTON. *(Mock weepy.)* Fine, but know this: You just might have been the one to change me. *(The dandy storms off. Kynaston smiles. Seven bells sound. Kynaston starts. He takes the letter from his bust. He looks at its contents. It's late. He looks around, lifts his skirts and runs off.)*

Scene 4

The stage of the Duke's Theater again. The bed, now without its curtains, is still center. It's late. Dark. No one to be seen. Outside noises of the London street. Maria enters the stage, whistling "The Willow Song" from Othello. *She carries a lantern. Maria looks at the bed. She picks up the red pillow. She inhales its scent. She looks around to see if the coast is clear. Then she performs the "murder scene" doing both roles, alas, neither very well.*

MARIA.
"Talk you of killing?"
(Deep voice.)
"Ay, I do."
(Her voice.)
"Alas, he is betray'd, and I undone!"
(Deep voice.)
"Down, strumpet!"
(Her voice.)
"Kill me to-morrow; let me live tonight!"
(Deep voice.)
"Nay, if you strive, —"
(Her voice.)
"But half an hour!"
(Deep voice.)
"Being done, there is no pause."
(Her voice.)
"But while I say one prayer!"
(Deep voice.)
"It is too late!"
(Maria falls back on the bed as if she's being smothered by the pillow. A noise off as Kynaston comes clattering onstage, out of breath. Maria leaps up. Brandishes lantern.) Who's th — ? *(Stops.)* Mr. Kynaston?
KYNASTON. Ohh ... God. No breath. Can't breathe. *(Holds side.)*
MARIA. Wound?
KYNASTON. *(Loosens sash around waist.)* Corset.
MARIA. What you doing out and about dressed like that?

KYNASTON. *(Huffing and puffing.)* Those two gentleladies who were here earlier wanted to feel me up for the sake of a wager. Help me with this, would you? *(Maria helps him undress.)*

MARIA. Yes, sir. Sir, the ladies … did they succeed?

KYNASTON. In what?

MARIA. In … "feeling" you.

KYNASTON. *(Smiles.)* What kind of girl do you take me for? *(Maria blushes, smiles.)* You're blushing.

MARIA. I am not!

KYNASTON. Then what makes your face so red in humour? *(Kynaston and Maria are looking at each other. Then Maria looks away.)*

MARIA. The lamp light. *(Gets back to work.)* Shall I wash your pillowcase?

KYNASTON. No. Let me die under it one more performance. You'd best head home. Get some sleep.

MARIA. … I'd sleep here if I could. *(Sits on bed.)* I'd sleep here tonight. *(Maria looks up at Kynaston. He gazes back at her, but gently declines her invitation.)*

KYNASTON. Maria, I shall not be charged with taking unfair advantage of womanly virtue. *(Pulls her up.)* I'll lock up when I'm done. Leave the lamp and go. Go, go, go!

MARIA. *(Sets lantern down.)* Watch the wick, sir. Don't burn yourself. *(Maria exits with the red pillow. Kynaston lets air escape his lungs. He sits on the bed starts to remove his shoes. And Villiars pops up from beneath the bed sheets.)*

VILLIARS. Milady.

KYNASTON. *(Leaps up.)* Damn!

VILLIARS. Scare you?

KYNASTON. Don't ever do that again.

VILLIARS. You were late. Thought I'd get in a quick nap. My note said seven, where were you?

KYNASTON. I was stranded in St. James' Park.

VILLIARS. What were you doing in St. James'?

KYNASTON. Two gentleladies offered me a shilling to touch my cock in front of their fathers.

VILLIARS. *(After a beat.)* This is why I prefer Hyde Park. So much less that sort of thing. So what happened?

KYNASTON. *(Takes wig off.)* We were interrupted by some frilly fop who thought we were whores on the make.

VILLIARS. St. James' is famous for its whores. Half the time, you can't see the forest for the bush. And this fop thought you were a woman?

KYNASTON. Once he felt the truth, off he went.

VILLIARS. Wasn't the case with me. *(Kynaston is in his shift now.)*

KYNASTON. *(Randy Desdemona voice.)* "Then, c'mon and give us a kiss."

VILLIARS. Not yet. Show you something. *(Digs in his cloak.)* Truth be told, I was late myself tonight.

KYNASTON. Dinner went long at Chesterfield's?

VILLIARS. I skipped Chesterfields. Pepys got to talking in the coach, tells me he's going to Killigrew's Theater tonight, something "surprising" that he didn't want to mention it in front of you and Betterton. So I tagged along. *(Takes out a flyer.)* Here's the fly-bill that was posted advertising the show.

KYNASTON. What is it?

VILLIARS. Read.

KYNASTON. *(Takes paper, reads.)*

"I come unknown to any of the rest
To tell you news: I saw the lady drest.
The woman plays today, mistake me not,
No man in gown or page in petticoat."

(Reads again.)

"The woman plays today."

(Puts down paper.) The woman.

VILLIARS. An act — tress.

KYNASTON. It's a joke. It's a fake. Jimmy Noakes, maybe or —

VILLIARS. I know Jimmy Noakes, and it was not Noakes, it was not any man. It was a girl.

KYNASTON. It's illegal.

VILLIARS. *(Shrugs.)* One did think as much.

KYNASTON. A woman playing a woman. What's the trick in that? What was the play?

VILLIARS. *Othello.*

KYNASTON. *(After a beat.)* … I take it the woman did not play the Moor.

VILLIARS. No.

KYNASTON. How was she?

VILLIARS. You mean the acting? Oh, I never notice the acting. But it reminded me of the first time I saw my estates. House falling down, gardens to seed, but all I could see were the possibilities.

KYNASTON. How'd she die?

VILLIARS. Sorry?

KYNASTON. When Desdemona died, how'd she, you know, get the pillow up her face?

VILLIARS. Rather quickly I thought. One, two, Desde's dead.

KYNASTON. You go backstage after?

VILLIARS. No. Green room was too crowded. Pepys went. If two mice were fucking in a nutshell he'd find room to squeeze in and write it down.

KYNASTON. What's her name? The "ac-tress."

VILLIARS. er ... Hughes. Pepys said she's mistress to some rich would-be. Going to be at the palace tonight. King's got a midnight supper and some singing thing.

KYNASTON. You invited?

VILLIARS. Yes.

KYNASTON. Are you going?

VILLIARS. If we finish up early, I might drop by.

KYNASTON. *(Strides away from Villiars.)* Oh, by all means, let's finish quick; I think that's rather your style. *(Beat.)*

VILLIARS. *(Dawns on him.)* ... You're jealous.

KYNASTON. *(Turns, scoffs.)* Of what?

VILLIARS. Well, I'm not sure.

KYNASTON. *(Paces, Trying to convince himself.)* This ac-tress ... it's a joke! A one-time thing! It's just ...

VILLIARS. What?

KYNASTON. *(Stops.)* Why did it have to be *Othello*? *(Turns to him.)* Do you love me?

VILLIARS. *(Smiles, comes to him.)* Where am I now? Who am I with now?

KYNASTON. Then take me ...

VILLIARS. *(Smiles, offers a hand.)* Come.

KYNASTON. ... to the palace.

VILLIARS. *(After a beat.)* What?

KYNASTON. I want to meet this "surprise."

VILLIARS. *(Chewing it over.)* You want to go to the palace?

KYNASTON. Yes.

VILLIARS. With me?

KYNASTON. Yes.

VILLIARS. As...?

KYNASTON. *(A hopeful smile.)* As your life's great love? *(Beat.)*

VILLIARS. You'll go as an "acquaintance" who behaves himself. And if you try to grow your part you'll find the role's been cut.

KYNASTON. To the palace then?

VILLIARS. No. First fuck, then see the freak. And Ned? Put this on? *(Holds up wig.)*
KYNASTON. *(After a beat.)* Would you ask your lady whores to wear a wig to bed?
VILLIARS. If it made them more a woman. Come on. I want to see a golden flow as I die in you. *(Kynaston picks up the wig and hands it to Villiars.)*
KYNASTON. "Will you to bed, my lord?"
VILLIARS. Ah, Desdemona. *(Kynaston sits on the bed. Villiars comes around the side of the bed and kneels on it above Kynaston. Villiars places the wig on Kynaston's head as if he is being crowned. Kynaston looks up at Villiars. They kiss. Then Kynaston lies down on the bed, his face facing out front.)* Die for me, Desdemona. *(The lantern remains on the stage floor. The two men begin to make love. After a moment, a shadow moves at the rear of the stage. A figure comes forward. It's Maria. She stays far upstage and holds on to the pillow. She buries her face in the pillow as she watches the love-making. The lantern lights goes out.)*

Scene 5

The court of King Charles II. A drum roll as Desdemona's bed goes off. An arras rises, revealing the opulent private mini-theatre of Charles II. A blast of period music. From the flies descends a beautiful woman in a gold helmet, purple plumage, gold shield and gold sword. As she descends, she sings. The singer is Nell Gwynn.

NELL.
  "Who can resist such mighty, mighty charms?
  Who can resist such mighty, mighty charms?
  Victorious!
  Victorious!
  Victorious love!
  Who can resist such mighty, mighty charms!
  And even the thunderer,
  The thunderer,

The thunderer love!
Who can resist such mighty charms?
Wo can resist such mighty, mighty charms?"
(Applause. King Charles II enters, resplendent. He claps for his mistress. Others hover and applaud. Charles II joins Nell on the tiny stage. We now glean that behind the gold shield she is completely naked but for high-heeled gold boots. [At best we see her bare bottom.])
CHARLES II. Brava, my dear! Well done! I think I can say with all certitude that was the finest, the most exquisite, the most perfectly sung and staged performance of "The Raging Dido" yet seen in the palace this week! *(Charles II grins and turns to his court. They clap again. Nell curtsies. Hyde, Charles' grim minister, enters. He is followed by Villiars and Kynaston. Both men are now in smart court dress.)*
HYDE. His Grace, the Duke of Buckingham, and Mr. Edward Kynaston.
CHARLES II. *(Grins.)* George!
VILLIARS. Majesty.
CHARLES II. *(Hugs him.)* George, where've you been? Thought you'd skipped us. *(To Kynaston.)* And ... Kynaston. Know you. You're —
NELL. *(Delighted.)* The actor!
CHARLES II. Ah! Would I have seen you in anything?
KYNASTON. I was in *Othello* this Thursday last at Mr. Betterton's.
CHARLES II. Who were you, Cassio? Roderigo? Not Iago, I hope, didn't like him.
KYNASTON. I played Desdemona.
CHARLES II. *(Awed.)* THAT Kynaston! Late the wife of the murderous Moor! Went to see the show last week, curtain was late, I said, "What's the matter," they said, "Your majesty, the Desdemona is still shaving!"
KYNASTON. You paint a blush upon me, Majesty.
CHARLES II. Long as you're not the Iago fellow, didn't like him in the least.
KYNASTON. His Highness may want to know our Iago is in fact a quite charming gentleman.
CHARLES II. I make no distinction between the part and its player, and neither I think does anyone else. Have you met Miss Gwynn, my Pretty Witty Nell?
NELL. Mr. Kynaston, I am a great admirer.
CHARLES II. Nell is the most ardent theatergoer in London.
NELL. I used to be an orange girl. I worked the stalls before, dur-

ing and after every performance. *(Shouts.)* "Oranges! Oranges! Two pence a pip!"

CHARLES II. *(Winces.)* Yes. *(Turns back to Kynaston.)* Kynaston, I was speaking to Betterton about *Othello* last week. Needs some changes. Mind you, it's first rate, but ... I don't know ... Could be ...

KYNASTON. Jollier?

NELL. That's what I said!

CHARLES II. The very word. I mean, what we want are —

KYNASTON. Surprises.

CHARLES II. Exactly.

NELL. But we don't want to know they're coming. *(Everyone turns to look at Nell.)*

KYNASTON. Er, we shall try our best when next you see the show. Day after tomorrow, yes? *(Hyde reenters.)*

HYDE. Mrs. Margaret Hughes.

CHARLES II. Heigh ho! Chock full of theatre folk. Swing her in. *(Margaret Hughes enters. Beautiful in a demure gown. Booming.)* Ahoy! Is this the face that launched a thousand claps? *(Margaret blushes.)*

HYDE. His Majesty refers to applause.

MARGARET. Majesty, I know not launches nor applause, but my little boat did make it 'cross rough seas and thankfully the claps were not of thunder.

CHARLES II. Now there's a entrance line! Mrs. Hughes, Miss Nell Gwynn.

NELL. I'd take your hand, but me tit would fall out.

CHARLES II. The Duke of Buckingham.

VILLIARS. Madame.

CHARLES II. And Mr. Kynaston, of the stage, like yourself.

MARGARET. Mr. Kynaston.

KYNASTON. *(Stiff now.)* Mrs. Hughes.

NELL. *(Excited whisper.)* Well? How was it?

MARGARET. The performance?

NELL. I wanted to see it, but we were doing this Dido thing. All that for a one off. Work, work, work, and it's over in a pop. Like Charlie. *(Laughs.)*

HYDE. Miss Gwynn, I remind you you are speaking of the father of his people.

NELL. Well, at least, a lot of 'em.

CHARLES II. Mrs. Hughes, was yours too a "one off?"

MARGARET. It certainly was novel. Whether Mr. Killigrew will repeat it, I cannot say.

28

VILLIARS. Well, I suppose it's a question of what the market will bear.

HYDE. And what the Crown will allow.

CHARLES II. My minister, Mr. Hyde is reminding me of my responsibilities as your sovereign.

HYDE. His Majesty has just this past week signed into law certain acts of restoration, although I doubt he is fully aware of all he has allowed and disallowed.

CHARLES II. It does no good to skimp in matters of reform. Out with the old, in with the new! I think it might be fun to see women on the stage. They've had them in France a long time now.

HYDE. *(Baleful.)* Yes, whenever we're about to do something truly horrible we always preface it by saying, "The French have been doing it for years."

KYNASTON. I hear there was a quite a crowd in your changing rooms tonight, Mrs. Hughes. His Grace the Duke said it was quite a mob scene.

HYDE. You see, Majesty? Mobs. Women on the stage beget disquiet.

NELL. Anybody important come?

MARGARET. I met a Mr. Pepys.

NELL. *(Rolls eyes.)* Oh.

MARGARET. You know him?

NELL. Got the pen marks on my arse to prove it.

MARGARET. *(To Villiars.)* If I may be so bold, your grace, seeing as you saw the performance … did you like it? *(All look at Villiars.)*

VILLIARS. *(The diplomat.)* I never tire of *Othello*.

KYNASTON. Truth be told, he never tires of Desdemona. Always sticking his head in. Last time we did it, he came 'round the back way.

VILLIARS. Actually, Mrs. Hughes I thought you showed a very pleasing Desdemona.

KYNASTON. But perhaps without quite the DEPTH he's accustomed to. *(Villiars glares at Kynaston.)*

MARGARET. Well, it was our first try. I hope we shall have more chances.

KYNASTON. Ah, well, that's the tricky thing about novelty. Do it more than once, it's not novel anymore.

MARGARET. That may be true, but in the theater I am told there are no old shows, Mr. Kynaston, just new audiences.

NELL. Charlie, let's see her!

CHARLES II. When can we go? Hyde?

HYDE. His Majesty is booked three weeks hence.

CHARLES II. Sorry, Nell.

VILLIARS. Well. *(Beat.)* If I may suggest, Your Majesty ... seeing as you've viewed Mr. Kynaston's Desdemona already ... why not see Mrs. Hughes' instead? I'm sure Mr. Kynaston would agree it's the collegial thing to do. *(Kynaston glares at Villiars.)*

CHARLES II. George, I'd make you a duke were you not a duke already. Make notes, Hyde.

HYDE. *(Jots.)* Saturday: *Othello.* The OTHER one.

CHARLES II. And now, forgive me, I have to pry our Midas from her prison de oro. Good to meet you, Mrs. Hughes.

NELL. *(To Margaret.)* Split an orange after. *(Nell and Charles exit. Hyde exits.)*

VILLIARS. Well, madam, will you excuse me, I think I see an acquaintance. I'll leave you to Mr. Kynaston to find ... more "depth." *(Villiars exits. Margaret and Kynaston are left alone. An uncomfortable pause. Then:)*

MARGARET. I have heard so much about you, Mr. Kynaston. I wish I could see YOUR Desdemona.

KYNASTON. Do you?

MARGARET. *(Quickly, nervous.)* Not that I consider Desdemona MINE, having made such brief and recent claim to her. But then a part doesn't belong to an actor, an actor belongs to a part, don't you agree? The portrait may be different, but the subject's the same. Still the same words. "I love you, I'm innocent, don't kill me, I'm dead."

KYNASTON. Tell me, Mrs. Hughes, how came you to play the role? Was it offered you by Mr. Killigrew?

MARGARET. I have a close acquaintance in a gentleman, Sir Charles Sedley, who has taken an interest in the theater. Mr. Killigrew's establishment needed certain financial situations set right, Sir Charles offered to patronize it. Consequently came the offer to perform.

KYNASTON. That's all it took?

MARGARET. That and an Act of Parliament.

KYNASTON. And how was the play itself chosen?

MARGARET. *(Nervous.)* The play?

KYNASTON. Yes. Why *Othello?*

MARGARET. Well ... the play does do well when it's performed, as you could attest. The plot, the bloodshed, the poetry.

KYNASTON. *Hamlet* has a plot.

MARGARET. Pardon me?

KYNASTON. Plenty of poetry in *Cymbeline.*

MARGARET. I —

KYNASTON. And surely the Scottish Play has bloodshed.

MARGARET. Oh, I'm far too young to play Lady — ! *(Stops herself, reverses gear.)* There was never a question, Mr. Kynaston. Desdemona is "the part." Oh, I do so wish you could see us play on Saturday. I'd love to know what you think of how I die!

KYNASTON. *(Smiles, purrs.)* Mrs. Hughes, I am always interested in how my rivals die *(Villiars returns.)*

VILLIARS. Ah, still talking shop. Mrs. Hughes, forgive me, did you know we had a friend in common?

MARGARET. And who is that, your grace. Surely you can't mean Mr. Kynaston?

VILLIARS. Your protector. We went to school together. *(Villiars gestures off. Sir Charles Sedley enters. He is the "dandy" Kynaston met in the park.)*

SEDLEY. Heigh-ho!

VILLIARS. Sir Charles Sedley, my good friend, may I present Mr. Edward Kynaston … an acquaintance.

SEDLEY. Kynaston. Odd. I have a feeling I've had the honor already.

KYNASTON. Or you've already had the honor of feeling it.

SEDLEY. *(Glassy-eyed.)* … I'm obviously behind in my drinking. Did you see my Pegs tonight, Kynaston?

KYNASTON. Otherwise engaged I fear.

MARGARET. Mr. Kynaston was himself being smothered by a man … IF I gleaned your meaning.

SEDLEY. Oh, yes, you're Betterton's Desdemona. You and Peg play the same part.

KYNASTON. But without the same parts.

SEDLEY. Well, you MUST see her Desdemona.

KYNASTON. Must I?

SEDLEY. Certainly. She's seen yours.

KYNASTON. *(Turns a wicked smile on her.)* Have you, Mrs. Hughes? You didn't tell me that. *(Margaret turns red.)*

SEDLEY. Copies you like a monk in cloister. Got so bad I told her she had to start acting more … manly. Fact is she saw you do the role so often, she said to me, "THAT is the role in which I must debut!" *(Margaret looks miserable. Kynaston smiles at her.)*

KYNASTON. My question is answered. Well, would that I could see her play me, but as we're opposites, I shan't have the chance.

SEDLEY. *(Eyes narrow.)* You won't go? Not even for the fun of it?

KYNASTON. Theater people don't go to plays for fun. We go to find out what went wrong. Besides, bad luck to watch a "colleague" play the same character whilst one is running. Who knows what good things one might wish to borrow, what others one might NOT.

VILLIARS. *(Tries to defuse.)* I'm heading home, Mr. Kynaston. Shall I DROP you?

KYNASTON. Yes, to bed, to bed. Tomorrow we audition new roles, then two shows of *The Silent Lady*. In it, I play a girl in a man's clothes. Might be your sort of thing, Mrs. Hughes. I'll look over the footlights, see if you're out there jotting notes. *(To Sedley.)* Sir Charles. *(Kynaston offers his hand to Sedley. Sedley shakes it coolly.)*

SEDLEY. Mr. Kynaston.

KYNASTON. *(Holds up glove, à la Sedley.)* I shall never wear this glove again! *(Sedley realizes who Kynaston is. Kynaston blows Sedley a kiss and exits grandly. Villiars, embarrassed, bows to Margaret and Sedley. Villiars exits.)*

SEDLEY. *(Glowering.)* This "Silent Lady" speaks too much. Mr. Kynaston is a fella in need of a come-down. And on his own turf. Did you tell him you're auditioning for Betterton tomorrow?

MARGARET. No.

SEDLEY. *(Smiles.)* Good. Surprise him.

MARGARET. Sir Charles, do you know Mr. Kynaston from before?

SEDLEY. Not really. Thought he was a whore tonight and grabbed his cock. *(They exit, arm in arm.)*

Scene 6

Backstage at the Duke's Theater. Three or four chairs are set. Maria ushers Nell into the scene. Nell is now well dressed. Maria is somewhat perplexed by Nell.

MARIA. Miss Gwynn. This is the stage.

NELL. *(Awed.)* Wo.

MARIA. You say you want to see Mr. Betterton?

NELL. Right. 'At's him.

MARIA. *(Bemused.)* I'll tell him you're here. *(Maria goes off. Nell looks around, awed. She grins and starts to spin in place like a little girl. Margaret enters, in a yellow cloak. Nell sees her and screams.)*

NELL. AHHHH! You scared me! I didn't know anybody was watchin'! Doncha recognize me, Mrs. Hughes! It's me! Nell!

MARGARET. *(Surprised.)* Miss Gwynn?

NELL. Surprised?

MARGARET. I am, yes.

NELL. Surprised meself! Didn't think I'd get up the nerve.

MARGARET. To...?

NELL. To audition! Don't tell Charlie. He knew I was here he'd bust a boil! Secret, eh?

MARGARET. What are you auditioning with?

NELL. What do you mean?

MARGARET. I mean what piece? For example, I have prepared a speech from a play.

NELL. *(Nods, uncomprehending.)* Clever idea. This speech, is it yours?

MARGARET. Well, it's Shakespeare's actually.

NELL. And he don't mind you using it?

MARGARET. I pray not.

NELL. I haven't done any speeches as yet, just songs. You got the speech written down?

MARGARET. No, I've memorized it from a prompt book.

NELL. Wo. That's hard. I don't read. You think that's a hindrance?

MARGARET. If you don't read, how do you memorize the words to the songs you sing?

NELL. Charlie makes the Prime Minister say the lyrics to me til I'm ready to kill him. After that, it just kind of sets in.

MARGARET. So what do you plan to do for your audition?

NELL. Well. First I thought I'd just sort of stand here for a while and let them have a good look — that's done surprisingly well for me to date. Next, I figured I'd sing a hymn about the temptation of Eve. Last, I take off my all of my clothes and pretend I'm wrestling a gigantic bulbous snake. It's worked before.

MARGARET. *(After a beat.)* How old are you, Miss Gwynn?

NELL. Fifteen.

MARGARET. No parents?

NELL. Me mum was a whore, me father the navy.

MARGARET. I see.

NELL. Yeah, that's why I don't never do sailors. Do you think they'll want a speech today?

MARGARET. I fear so.

NELL. I knew I forgot something. I mean, I want to be an actress more 'n anything, but if I got to READ ... Here, now I've got flies in my gullet. I gotta do a run. Save me place?

MARGARET. Of course.

NELL. *(Stands, hesitates.)* Friends for life?

MARGARET. Run of the show. *(Nell smiles, then dashes off. Betterton enters, dressed in the armor of some great military figure — very much the fat, male version of what Nell wore in her performance in "The Raging Dido.")*

BETTERTON. *(Calls off.)* Maria! MARIA! Damnit, girl, where are you?! Fucking codpiece is half way up my fundament! *(Sees Margaret.)* Ho! Who are you?

MARGARET. *(Stands.)* Mr. Betterton, I am Margaret Hughes. I am here to audition.

BETTERTON. *(Perplexed.)* As what?

MARGARET. As an actress.

BETTERTON. Dear girl, we do not employ actresses. Now it's almost curtain! Scurry off, we have a show to — *(Betterton starts off, stops, turns.)* Hang on. "Margaret Hughes?" The Hughes who played last night at Killigrew's?

MARGARET. Yes, that was I.

BETTERTON. *(Comes to her.)* Heavens. Everyone's talking about last night's performance and your appearance in it.

MARGARET. Good words, I hope.

BETTERTON. Well, they're talking, that's the main thing. Killigrew going to perform it again?

MARGARET. Tomorrow night.

BETTERTON. Then, he has you to a contract?

MARGARET. I have signed no contract as there is no assurance of future opportunities. Mr. Killigrew has been most kind, but … I have always been desirous of working at your theater. I've seen you and Mr. Kynaston dozens of times. You're my favorite theater couple! *(Kynaston enters, dressed as a fop with long red hair.)*

KYNASTON. Tommy— *(Sees her.)* Mrs. Hughes.

MARGARET. Mr. Kynaston.

BETTERTON. You've met?

MARGARET. We've exchanged words.

KYNASTON. Are we giving tours, Tommy?

BETTERTON. Mrs. Hughes is desirous of an audition as today has been our day to see players. Pray, do you have a scene for us, Mrs. Hughes?

MARGARET. I do, actually.

KYNASTON. Tommy, it's but a few minutes to curtain —

MARGARET. It won't take but a minute. *(Kynaston fumes. Betterton decides.)*

BETTERTON. Mrs. Hughes. Take the stage. *(The men sit. Margaret starts to move the auditioner's chair. Betterton hops up and moves it for her.)* Allow me. *(Holds chair for her, as she sits.)*

MARGARET. *(Sits.)* My thanks.

BETTERTON. *(Bows, smiles.)* My pleasure. *(Betterton sits next to Kynaston.)*

BETTERTON. What, Mrs. Hughes, will you be doing for us today?

MARGARET. A soliloquy.

BETTERTON. From?

MARGARET. *(Hesitates.)* ... *Othello.*

BETTERTON. ... And the role?

MARGARET. *(Nervous.)* ... Desdemona.

BETTERTON. *(Glances at Kynaston.)* Well, then, this should be fun.

MARGARET.
  "What shall I do to win my lord again?
    Good friend, go to him; for by this light of heaven,
    I know not how ... "
(She stops. She winces and makes a pleading face.) May I start over?

BETTERTON. *(Unctuous.)* Please.

MARGARET. Thank you.
  "What shall I do to win my lord again?
    Good friend, go to him; for by this light of heaven,
    I know not how ...
    I know not how ... "

KYNASTON. "I know not how I lost him."

MARGARET. *(Tight.)* My thanks.

KYNASTON. My pleasure. I say it every night.

MARGARET. May I begin again?

BETTERTON. Heavens, I was going to suggest it myself!

KYNASTON. "I know not how—"

MARGARET *(Loud; red faced anger.)* " — I-know-not-how-I-lost-him! *(What follows is a ghastly rendering of the speech. Every mistake an actress can make, Margaret makes. Lots of gestures, histrionics, too fast, too slow. It's a classic.)*

MARGARET.
  "What shall I do to win my lord again?
    Good friend, go to him; for by this light of heaven,
    I know not how I lost him.
    Here I kneel.

If e'er my will did trespass 'gainst his love,
Either in discourse of thought
Or actual deed
Or that mine eyes, mine ears, or any sense *(Sniffs.)*
Delighted them in any other form;
Or that I do not yet, and ever did,
And ever will — though he do shake me off
To beggarly divorcement — love him dearly,
Comfort forswear me! Unkindness may do much,
And his unkindness may defeat my life,
But never taint my love." *(Stops.)*
That was it.

BETTERTON. *(Stunned.)* ... Yes, of course it was! Sorry, I was so ... caught up in the ... gestures and such. Well. I have never heard the role performed quite that way before.

MARGARET. Do you think there might be something for me?

BETTERTON. Don't know. Depends.

MARGARET. On?

KYNASTON. *(Deadpan.)* On hundreds if not thousands of actors ahead of you dying of the plague.

BETTERTON. Ned's being funny —

KYNASTON. *(Stands.)* It depends on the audiences of London losing their eyes, their ears, and truth be told, their sense of *(Sniffs à la Margaret.)* ... smell. I must confess, Mrs. Hughes, when I heard about your performance at Killigrew's last night, I was worried! I thought: Women on the stage, what will become of me? And then you auditioned for us! You have taken a great load off my mind.

MARGARET. *(Hurt and stiff.)* I take it the answer is no.

BETTERTON. *(Solicitous.)* We'll keep in touch. Best of luck tomorrow night. Wish I could slip in and see.

MARGARET. *(Eyes welling, starts off.)* I would arrange tickets, but we're sold out.

BETTERTON. *(Light bulb!)* Sold out?

MARGARET. *(Starts to cry.)* Yes!

BETTERTON. Sold out every seat?

MARGARET. *(Crying.)* Since last night Mr. Killigrew's been getting requests apace!

BETTERTON. Requests apace. You mean: SALES IN ADVANCE? Mrs. Hughes, you say Mr. Killigrew has not signed a contract with you.

MARGARET. *(Turns, sniffs.)* Not as yet, although he made mention last night —

BETTERTON. Whatever he offered, I'll double it! Ned! What say we brought in Mrs. Hughes to play one of the roles? "Emilia" perhaps? Or "Bianca?" Not "you-know-who," of course, that's you, but — splash things up a bit. What do you think?

KYNASTON. I refuse.

BETTERTON. What do you mean "refuse"?

KYNASTON. I shall not act with her.

BETTERTON. By what right?

KYNASTON. My rights. Mr. Betterton, you gave me approval over casting. And I hereby exercise said rights.

BETTERTON. But she's sold out Killigrew's!

MARGARET. *(Trying to convince Ned.)* Indeed! The theater was packed and the crowd clapped and clapped!

KYNASTON. I recall a puppet show once where a recently departed dog was stuffed and made to dance with Punch and Judy, and that crowd was packed and clapping too.

MARGARET. Do you mean to be quite so insulting, sir, or is it just your nature?

KYNASTON. A feminine prerogative.

MARGARET. At least I am what I appear to be, instead of some mincing catamite!

KYNASTON. Madam I have worked half my life to do what I do! Fourteen boys in a cellar, crammed in with a former boy player who pawed at us day and night. A fat old fellow who'd take in urchins like me and teach us the tricks and turns. It was all completely illegal, of course, Cromwell being the theater fan he was, but that Old Boy, he'd whisper in my ear, "Mark me, the stage'll come back, and when it does, my lad, you'll be its star." What teacher did YOU learn from? What cellar was YOUR home?

MARGARET. *(Cold.)* I had no teacher nor such a classroom, but then I had less need of training. *(We hear a chant begin.)*

OFFSTAGE VOICES. Start the play! Start the play! Start the play!

BETTERTON. Ned, this lady …

KYNASTON. *(To Betterton.)* Mr. Betterton, if you insist on arguing the case for Mrs. Hughes further — indeed if you attempt to audition her or any other women ever again — I will consider it a breech of contract, and leave the stage forthwith. Now, do we play or do you refund the house? *(We hear feet stomping in their seats.)*

OFFSTAGE VOICES. Start the play! Start the play! Start the play!

(Betterton glares.)

BETTERTON. *(A chilled voice.)* I am a man of my contract and my word. You exercise your rights today, I mine tomorrow

KYNASTON. *(Bows.)* Thank you, Mr Betterton. I shall await my cue. *(Kynaston sweeps off. Betterton fumes. Nell rushes onstage.)*

NELL. God, I must've dropped ten stone! Is this Mr. Betterton?

MARGARET. *(Low and sad.)* Mr. Betterton cannot audit today.

NELL. What? *(The offstage chants are louder now.)*

BETTERTON. It's too late. The curtain must rise.

NELL. *(Red eyed.)* But — I hurried fast as I could! What about after the play?

BETTERTON. No.

NELL. Then tomorrow — ?

MARGARET. *(Defeated.)* He cannot audit you at all, Miss Gwynn.

BETTERTON. I fear I gave Mr. Kynaston approval over my players, and Mr. Kynaston refuses to see players who are of the feminine form. *(Chants offstage louder. Nell's tears freeze to anger.)*

NELL. *(Snarls.)* BITCH! *(To Betterton.)* Does he know who I am?

BETTERTON. Madame, whoever you are, it is enough for Mr. Kynaston that you are a woman!

NELL. *(Fury.)* Well, mark me, sir! Women shall lay blame for this! *(Nell grabs Margaret and storms off. The chants are raging.)*

OFFSTAGE VOICES. Start the play! Start the play! Start the play!

BETTERTON. Places! Curtain up!

(Betterton exits. Three knocks of the cane. Curtain rises. Footlights come up. Kynaston strolls on, dressed in his "britches" garb.)

AUDIENCE. Ahhhhh! *(Applause.)*

KYNASTON.

"Come I to London
  At seventeen,
  But wait, don't speak
  Til you have seen
  The locks that fall from neath my hat
  I am a girl
  And that is that!
  Dressed as a man to find my fortune,
  A babe on a doorstep,
  A bastard orphan
  Here to seek my wealth and fame,
  And needs be I must change my na — "

(Audience voice calls out.)

VOICE 1. BUM BOY!

KYNASTON. *(Halts a moment.)* " — my name — "

VOICE 1. BUM BOY! ARSE LICKER!

KYNASTON. *(Tries to compose himself.)* … Methinks a wit is in the house tonigh —

VOICE 1. SHOW US YOUR TEETH! LET'S SEE THE SHIT ON YOUR TEETH!

VOICE 2. LET'S SEE THE BLACK WHERE YE CHEW THE DUKE'S RANK ARSE!

VOICE 1.
>WHAT'D THEY DO.
>WITH YOUR SMALL PRICK?

VOICE 2.
>THEY WHACKED IT OFF.
>TO DO THE TRICK!

(More laughter. Kynaston steps back from the footlights as a small wet burlap bag filled with something hits the stage.)

VOICE 1. Lubricator for your well and drill.

VOICE 2. Shit for a shit-bum boy! *(Kynaston peers at the bag, then recoils, pulls out his handkerchief and puts it to his nose. More laughter.)*

VOICE 3.
>HEY NON NONNY
>WHAT'S NORTH AND SOUTH
>A FACE IN HIS ARSE
>AND AN ARSE IN HIS MOUTH!

(Whoops of laughter as another bag hits the stage.)

VOICE 2.
>NED THEY CALL HIM
>HERMAPRHODITE
>HIS PRICK'S ALWAYS BURIED
>WHERE IT'S OPEN ALL NIGHT!

(Cheers and laughter as more bags hit the stage. Kynaston falls. Maria comes onstage to help him to his feet. They go off through one of the two onstage doors as wild cheers come from the audience!)

BETTERTON. Bring the curtain down! *(Their prey has been driven from the stage. The cheers die.)*

Scene 7

The green room. Betterton — still in costume, but without his helmet — strides in. He paces, wringing his hands. Kynaston enters slowly with Maria. His wig and hat are gone. His clothes are splotched with brown smears. Maria hovers behind him, holding a cloth with which she has obviously been trying to clean him. Maria tries to wipe some of the shit from Kynaston's face, but he jerks his face away from her. Maria rushes offstage. Kynaston makes his way to his make-up table. Betterton wrinkles his nose and backs away from him, both to avoid being smeared himself and to give Kynaston's anger its room to breathe. The cheers have by now faded to silence.

BETTERTON. I, uh, think it would be best if we did not perform the second show. I don't want a repetition of THIS! I'll tell the box office to refund the tickets.

KYNASTON. Nonsense. We're going to play to a full house tonight.

BETTERTON. What makes you think that?

KYNASTON. Because the "wits" of the town are even now sitting in their coffee houses telling what happened to Ned Kynaston when he played *The Silent Lady* today. And what will happen to him when he plays her next.

BETTERTON. I can't allow it. The things they threw on the stage could have been bricks or glass or —

KYNASTON. It was shit. *(Maria enters.)*

MARIA. A letter, Mr. Kynaston. *(Hands it to him.)* No perfume. *(Kynaston opens it, reads silently.)*

BETTERTON. What is it?

KYNASTON. It's a poem.
  "ONSTAGE WOMEN ARE SO SIZED
   YOU'D THINK THEY WERE THE GUARD DISGUISED;
   WITH BONE SO LARGE AND INCOMPLIANT
   CALL DESDEMONA, ENTER GIANT."
From Sir Charles Sedley.

BETTERTON. Why's he sending you doggerel?

KYNASTON. He's serving notice. It was he paid the ruffians to smear me with verse and shit.

BETTERTON. *(Points at letter.)* Does he say as much?

KYNASTON. No.

BETTERTON. Then how do you know he authored their barbs?

KYNASTON. The rhyme scheme is the same. This is his repayment for my refusal to act with his whore, the Hughes. *(Soft, like a small child, a chant.)* Why are they doing this to me? Why are they doing this to me? Why — ?

BETTERTON. Ned…? *(Pause.)*

KYNASTON. *(Determined.)* We shall play tonight.

BETTERTON. Ned —

KYNASTON. To a full house. And we'll beat Sir Charles and his whore who came to you today. I insist.

BETTERTON. *(Seethes.)* You'll insist yourself to hell, Mr. Kynaston. *(Betterton goes off. Kynaston stares out at his image in the mirror, Maria behind him.)*

KYNASTON. Yes, I probably will. *(Maria starts off.)* Maria, don't go. Plots must I lay, deceptions treacherous. *(Gets an idea.)* I must prove a villain to foil a villain.

MARIA. *(Doesn't get it.)* Sir…?

KYNASTON. *(Stands.)* I think these clothes have seen better days! In *The Silent Lady*, I play a woman playing a man, yes?

MARIA. A "dandy" of the town.

KYNASTON. Well, then, here's what I need: *(Kynaston grabs Maria by the hand, pulls her up and sweeps her off with him. Lights dim slightly on the green room as lights come up on another part of the stage. A beat later, King Charles II descends from the flies in Nell's chariot. He's in a long dressing gown, reading papers. Nell is sniffling dramatically, hoping to gain Charles' attention. Charles does indeed look up from his papers and sees Nell before him.)*

CHARLES II. Nelly? Is that you?

NELL. *(Black mood.)* Yes!

CHARLES II. What is it, sweets? You been crying? *(Nell looks up at Charles and breaks into fresh tears.)*

NELL. Charlie? You'd help me to do what I want, wouldn't you?

CHARLES II. I've always said.

NELL. And you'd never deny me?

CHARLES. *(After a beat — suspicious.)* What do you want? *(Nell stands and goes to Charles. He bends to her as she whispers. Charles suddenly pulls back from whatever Nell has whispered. He looks*

41

shocked.) Nell! I can't.

NELL. *(Pleading.)* Charlie —

CHARLES. *(Shakes head.)* It's out of the question.

NELL. I'll never ask another favor —

CHARLES II. No!

NELL. *(A dirty leer.)* Charlie … *(Nell starts to slide down his front.)*

CHARLES II. Here now, Nell, I've work to do — *(Nell starts to undo Charles' belt.)*

NELL. Charlie-Boy, where's his toy…?

CHARLES II. Nelly, this is important stuff — taxes and knighthoods, we're at war with the Dutch.

NELL. Your Majesty, let me see the Crown! *(Nell dives beneath his robes. She disappears inside the folds of the dressing gown. His eyes roll back.)*

CHARLES II. OH! OHHHHH! OHHHH, NELLY! *(Charles comes. Nell looks up and whistles. The chariot ascends with the happy Charles carried aloft. Nell dabs her lips, smiles, and exits demurely. Simultaneous to their exit, sound up: an audience before the curtain goes up. Lights rise on an area representing the upper boxes of the theater. Sedley appears in the "box." Margaret appears with him.)*

SEDLEY. *(Smug.)* Mrs. Hughes. How went the audition?

MARGARET. *(Still steaming, but she lies.)* … I did not come here. I had a headache.

SEDLEY. Pity, I've been here most of the day to see Mr. Kynaston play.

MARGARET. *(Bitter.)* Did he play WELL?

SEDLEY. He did not play LONG.

MARGARET. *(Suspects something.)* What happened?

SEDLEY. *(Sneers.)* It was critics' day. *(Pepys enters, out of breath. He looks around. Sedley sees Pepys and waves at him. Villiars enters.)*

SEDLEY. Pepys! Your Grace!

PEPYS. *(Looks up.)* Sir Charles!

SEDLEY. You got my message, then?

PEPYS. I came as soon as I received your cryptic invitation. *(Looks around.)*

VILLIARS. You have assembled quite a theater party, Sir Charles.

SEDLEY. I have invited the cream of London society to join us this evening.

PEPYS. Well, I am grateful to be included, although I must confess, I have seen *The Silent Lady* a good few times before.

SEDLEY. Not as you shall tonight. That's why I most particularly wanted you here.

PEPYS. To what end?

SEDLEY. Why, Mr. Pepys, to write it down. For posterity. *(Three knocks of the cane. Pepys sits. Sedley and Margaret look at the stage. Lights dim as the lights brighten on the stage. The curtain rises and we see Kynaston center, dressed exactly as Sedley: cane, hat, gloves, colors, everything. He faces out front.)*

KYNASTON.

"Come I to London
At seventeen,
But wait, don't speak
Til you have seen
The locks that fall from neath my hat
I am a fop
And that is that!
Dressed as a man, I seek a verse
To sing the praise
Of one who's worse
Than any dandy, fool
Or fraud
Dressed as a clown
And shoddily shod.
No barbs hurled here
Can ere compare
To this knight's barbarous
Verse, I dare;
So here proclaim a scathing medley
Of this poor dolt, so dull and deadly
A man whose lisp pronounced him "Thedley."
That oafish prick,
Our own Charles Sedley."

(Audience whoops with laughter and applause as Kynaston bows. Margaret looks embarrassed. Sedley looks aghast. Pepys stands and claps. Cheers go on and on!)

Scene 8

Backstage. The green room. The action is continuous. Sedley has stormed off, with Margaret exiting soon thereafter. Kynaston, triumphant, enters. He removes his hat. Pepys and Villiars are waiting for him. Pepys looks ecstatic. Villiars betrays no expression. Betterton and Maria enter.

PEPYS. Bravo, Mr. K.! Bravo! There was the house, full to the brim with the all best society above and there below three or four ruffian sorts with somewhat smelly bags between them. And then the curtain rised and you appeared. I have never heard such an intake of breath; the candle fire was almost sucked into our breasts! And as you spoke, the laughter came, and I stole a glance at Sedley's face, but there was no mirth in it. Even his ruffian boys with their sacks laughed and mocked him. It was the finest night I've ever had in the theater!

BETTERTON. How'd you like the play?

PEPYS. Oh, fuck the play.

KYNASTON. *(Takes Maria's hand.)* It's Maria's doing. Maria has the eye and the hand.

MARIA. You inspired me, sir.

KYNASTON. *(Kisses Maria's hand.)* And you me. What say I take you to dinner, eh?

MARIA. Dinner?

KYNASTON. Yes. *(To Villiars.)* What do you say, Your Grace? Shall we both escort our genius girl to dine?

VILLIARS. *(Cool.)* I fear I cannot, Mr. Kynaston. *(Lady Meresvale and Miss Frayne enter.)*

KYNASTON. Ah. Well, then. *(To Maria.)* It's you and me then.

LADY MERESVALE. Mr. Kynaston.

KYNASTON. Ah. Lady Meresvale. Miss Frayne. Come to see if I'm really Sir Charles Sedley? You can take a look in my head, you'll find no brain.

LADY MERESVALE. Mr. Kynaston, we wish to apologize for our rudeness yesterday afternoon. We wish to make things up with you. May we take you to a supper at Chesterfield's?

KYNASTON. *(After a pause.)* Well. Why not? Dressed as I am, I may commit any crime, and lay the fault at the door of the dullard dandy. *(Kynaston and the ladies sweep off.)*

PEPYS. *(Calling after them.)* Good night, Mr. K.! Bravo again! *(To Betterton.)* All's well that ends well! Eh?

BETTERTON. Let's hope so. Whorehouse?

PEPYS. Whorehouse. *(Betterton and Pepys exit. Villiars looks at Maria. She is staring after Kynaston, her eyes red.)*

VILLIARS. You crying?

MARIA. *(Looks away.)* No, sir. It's the lamp-light. Will ... will you be back again to see the show tomorrow?

VILLIARS. *(After a beat.)* No. I have had my fill of Desdemona. *(Villiars exits.)*

MARIA. *(Simply.)*
    "What shall I do to win my lord again?
    For by this light of heaven,
    I know not how I lost him."
(Maria begins to cry. Lights fade.)

Scene 9

The park. The ladies and Kynaston enter again.

LADY MERESVALE. Oh, let's stop ... here, why don't we.

KYNASTON. Don't tell me the Earl of Lauderdale and the Wigmaster are in the upper window again. *(Miss Frayne and Lady Meresvale exchange a look.)*

MISS FRAYNE. No.

LADY MERESVALE. Tarry a while, Mr. Kynaston. Flatter me, who does not deserve your good graces.

KYNASTON. Very well. *(Lady Meresvale slaps Kynaston.)*

LADY MERESVALE. You mocked us, sir. You, an actor, mocked your betters!

MISS FRAYNE. Hit him again!

LADY MERESVALE. You shall know the other end of it now, shit-boy! *(Three ruffians appear out of the darkness. One from upstage center, One from stage left. One from stage right. Each carries a cudgel or stick.)*

RUFFIAN 1. Look 'ere.

RUFFIAN 2. A dandy.

RUFFIAN 3. A frothy boy spun in sugar!

RUFFIAN 1. Ere wait, I know this one.

RUFFIAN 2. Me too.

RUFFIAN 3. It's Sir Charles Sedley.

KYNASTON. You mistake me, gentlemen.

RUFFIAN 2. No mistake.

RUFFIAN 1. Tis he. The Sedley.

RUFFIAN 3. Dressed as we had been foretold.

RUFFIAN 1. You did ignite certain respected lords and ladies,sir.

RUFFIAN 2. We have been procured to pronounce the penalty.
(Ruffian 1 swings his stick and slams it into Kynaston's belly. Lights change. Kynaston is beaten by the ruffians in slow motion as the ladies watch, fanning themselves with their fans. As the beating goes on, Charles II enters with a few pieces of paper. He speaks out front as if to an audience of politicians.)

CHARLES II.   Ministers of the Privy Council! I present to Parliament an Edict which I wish to have passed, put down in law and posted throughout the effected areas post-haste. *(Kynaston continues to be beaten. Pepys enters with his diary.)*

PEPYS. "December 10, 1661. To the theater this afternoon to see again *The Moor of Venice*, and found the theater closed, the play postponed. Apparently, Mr. Kynaston met with an accident in the park last night and is not recovered to play. So off to Covent Garden where I did see posted an edict newly issued from the King. A licensing law which states in binding language as does follow: "Whereas the women's parts in plays have hitherto been acted by men in the habits of women, at which some have taken offense, we do permit and give leave for the time to come, that all women's parts be acted by women. No He shall ere again upon an English stage play She." *(Lights narrow to Kynaston on the ground; then to a spot on Kynaston's hand. It is bloody and clutches a handkerchief. It twitches in the light. Black out.)*

End of Act One

ACT TWO

Scene 1

Pepys in front of the curtain.

PEPYS. "To the theater to see a play ... " *(Sound: Music underscores the following.)* " ... The King's edict passed, Mr. Betterton has been forced to find his ladies elsewhere." *(Curtain rises. We see Betterton onstage with Maria. He holds a pillow. They are rehearsing.)*
MARIA. "Talk you of killing?"
BETTERTON. "Ay, I do."
MARIA. "O, banish me, my lord, but kill me not!"
BETTERTON. "Down, strumpet!"
MARIA. "Kill me to-morrow; let me live tonight!"
BETTERTON. "Nay, if you strive — "
MARIA. "But while I say one prayer!"
BETTERTON. "It is too late!" *(Betterton puts the pillow over Maria's face.)* Thunder, thunder, thunder. *(Maria peeks out from behind the pillow.)*
MARIA. *(Meek.)* Better?
BETTERTON. *(Winces.)* Let's do it again. *(They start off.)*
MARIA. "Talk you of killing?"
BETTERTON. *(Meaning it.)* "Ay, I do." *(They have exited.)*
PEPYS. "Upon inquiry, am told Mr. Kynaston has not played these six weeks passed, his injuries still not having healed. And so to the Law Courts where the trial of the three ruffians who did batter Mr. K. takes place." *(Ruffians enter.)* "But the ruffians' reply to the court is ... "
RUFFIANS. We thought he was Sir Charles Sedley.
PEPYS. " ... whose image Mr. K. had most undoubtably imitated." *(Sedley enters in his dandy clothes.)* "And as Mr. K. does not appear in court ... the ruffians go free." *(Ruffians exit, Sedley gives them each a coin.)* "And so with the triumphant Sedley to the Royal Gallery, where his mistress, Mrs. Hughes, sits for the portraitist,

Lelly." *(Margaret enters and poses. Lelly enters.)* "Sir Charles has commissioned the painting in the hopes of making quite a stir. But the sitting is not going well."

LELLY. Mrs. Hughes, if I am to paint the first actress on the English stage, I must paint her with tits exposed. How else prove to the public she is really a woman?!

MARGARET. I want to be taken as a serious actress!

SEDLEY. Madam, before you can be taken seriously, you must put bums in seats! *(Margaret fumes, then pulls down part of her dress to reveal one of her breasts.)*

MARGARET. Paint quickly. It's cold as — it's cold. *(Lelly backs away, in awe. He smacks his lips.)*

PEPYS. "And thus is art made flesh." *(Margaret exits, as Lelly and Sedley follow.)* "After which to Covent Garden to inquire if the Duke of Buckingham will join me at the theater ... " *(Villiars enters with Lady Meresvale and Miss Frayne. Villiars whispers into Lady Meresvale's ear. She blushes.)*

LADY MERESVALE. Ohhhh!

PEPYS. " ... but the Duke has of late abandoned painted back-drops for less dimensional pursuits." *(Villiars and Lady Meresvale exit in one direction.)*

MISS FRAYNE. *(Pouts.)* Ohhh! *(Miss Frayne exits in the other.)*

PEPYS. "Afterwhich, to the Palace." *(Charles II enters.)*
" ... where the King hosts a birthday celebration for himself."

CHARLES II. Happy birthday to me. *(The chariot of Dido descends. It's garish and over-the-top. It carries Nell, in full regalia.)*

PEPYS. "The hostess is Nell, whose talents have grown by such leaps and bounds she has decided to author her own birthday verse to the King."

NELL. *(Spoken.)*
    "'To our Great Mars
      From his Sweet Venus:
      Here's to the Crown
      And here's to His Penis.'"
(Chariot, Nell, and Charles exit. The music is over.)

PEPYS. "And so at long last at the end of a full and busy day ... to the coffee house to sift and sort the wit and wisdom of the sun and moon just past." *(A coffee bar slides in. Pepys sits with his diary and sips coffee. A man enters. He wears a plain dark suit. He wears sunglasses and needs the cane with which he supports himself. It's Kynaston.)* Mr. K.? 'Tis I. Pepys. *(Kynaston removes his sunglasses. His eyes are bruised and red.)*

48

KYNASTON. Pepys. Hardly recognized you without your book.

PEPYS. And I you without your — well, you don't look yourself. Sit, sit.

KYNASTON. I mustn't.

PEPYS. No, please.

KYNASTON. No, really.

PEPYS. I insist.

KYNASTON. *(Firm.)* Better I stand.

PEPYS. Of course. Bad for the back, eh? Should have realized. You're on the mend though?

KYNASTON. Every day.

PEPYS. Back on stage soon?

KYNASTON. Soon as they'll let me.

PEPYS. Physicians, eh? What role will mark your return?

KYNASTON. What else but Desdemona?

PEPYS. *(A beat.)* ... Ah. *(Changes gears.)* You know, Mr. K., the performance of yours I always liked best? Well, as much as I adored your Desdemona and your Juliet, I always loved best the "britches" parts. Rosalind, f'rinstance. And not just because of the woman stuff, but also because of the man sections. Your performance of the man stuff seemed so right, so true, that I suppose I felt it was the most real in the play.

KYNASTON. You know why the man stuff seems real? Because I'm pretending. You see a man through the mirror of a woman through the mirror of a man; take one of those reflecting glasses away and it doesn't work; the man only works because you see him in contrast to the woman he is; if you saw him without the her he lives inside, he wouldn't seem a man at all.

PEPYS. *(Blinks at that.)* You have obviously thought longer on this question than I. Well. *(Stands.)* Must home to my wife. Pleasure to see you, Mr. K.

KYNASTON. Have you finished your coffee?

PEPYS. ... er ... yes. Would you ... like to drink it?

KYNASTON. I'd like to clear it. *(Pepys stares as Kynaston takes a white apron from his pocket and places it around his waist. He then leans over and takes the coffee cup.)*

PEPYS. Ah. Thank you. *(Beat — takes out a coin.)* May I — ?

KYNASTON. *(Takes coin.)* Thank you, sir. A pleasant evening, sir. Come again. *(Kynaston limps off behind the bar with the coffee. Pepys stares another moment. Then he exits.)*

Scene 2

A bare stage. Upstage center, Betterton enters, carrying the figure of a woman in his arms. He staggers downstage to the footlights. Betterton carries a life-size female doll, the kind made of horse-hair and cotton. No features on the doll's face. It wears a white shift. Betterton mouths a speech as he hoists the doll and kisses its face. Kynaston has remained onstage. He watches Betterton.

KYNASTON. Lear.

BETTERTON. *(Starts, then turns to see him.)* How'd you guess?

KYNASTON. *(Indicates the doll.)* Cordelia. You're practicing your carry. *(Comes over to the doll — lifts it.)* Light.

BETTERTON. Lighter than you. Although the distribution of weight somehow makes it clumsier. *(Betterton sets the doll down in a corner.)*

KYNASTON. *(Points at doll.)* That work in performance?

BETTERTON. It's for rehearsal. In performance I carry a real woman.

KYNASTON. And that is?

BETTERTON. Maria.

KYNASTON. *(Taken aback.)* ... Any good?

BETTERTON. Surprisingly effective in her lack of affectation. Only trouble is the last scene. I'm hovering over her body, moaning, "Never, never, never," and she's trying to stitch up my hem. Once a seamstress ... Why'd you want to see me?

KYNASTON. *(Smiles.)* Pick me up, see how light I am. *(A bit of doggerel.)*
  "Carry me to the chamber,
    Fling me on the bed,
    Lament my tragic death,
    Put a pillow 'pon my head."

BETTERTON. Can't. Crown'll close me if I do. 'Sides, the company's full-up. You weren't the only actor cut loose by the Law. Town's full of your sort now, begging for crumbs. Doing *Hamlet* next week, forty-seven men auditioned for *Osric, the Courtier*. Jimmy Noakes got the part. I said, "Jimmy, you played concubines

50

and queens, why go out for Osric? He says, "Darling, he's the closest thing." How the mighty are fallen. I'm being unkind ... on purpose. You cost me the palace's support. You stopped my theater seeing actresses the day the King's mistress came to audition. That edict was Nell Gwynn's revenge upon us all. I struggle now. I grovel to the King and Miss Gwynn at every chance. Slowly, ice melt by ice melt, they soften. Take you back would freeze me out again. *(Beat.)* Did you try Killigrew?

KYNASTON. Killigrew employs Peg Hughes, whom, if I saw, I would be duty bound to strangle. Tommy? Is she any good as an actress?

BETTERTON. *(Shrugs.)* She's a star. She did what she did first. And you did what you did last. *(Betterton scoops up the doll and exits.)*

Scene 3

The Turkish baths. Steam. Sound of hissing. A marble bench comes downstage center. A coat tree with hooks for towels and a lavish robe is set next to it. Villiars, a towel around his waist, is seated on the bench ... He's sweating. He throws his head back. He closes his eyes. Kynaston has remained onstage. He turns upstage to see Villiars. Villiars senses him and looks up.

VILLIARS. Good God. You'll poach in that.

KYNASTON. *(Chilly.)* Would your grace like me to disrobe?

VILLIARS. *(Looks around.)* Quiet! This isn't the place.

KYNASTON. I thought you hated heat and steam.

VILLIARS. I am purifying myself. I want to purge all evils from my pores.

KYNASTON. That include me? *(A man enters. He's the bath club bouncer.)*

BOUNCER. Sir, are you a member of the club?

VILLIARS. *(A glance at Kynaston.)* ... He's my guest of the moment.

BOUNCER. Yes, Your Grace. *(Bouncer eyes Kynaston and leaves.)*

VILLIARS. *(A snarled whisper.)* Any more of that I'll have you taken bodily!

KYNASTON. Not the first time. *(Moves closer.)* Why didn't you

51

come to my rooms when you heard I'd been attacked?

VILLIARS. *(Swallows.)* I knew you wouldn't WANT me to see what they'd done to you.

KYNASTON. *(After a beat.)* Why didn't you write?

VILLIARS. *(Looks away.)* Ned, I've never been a word-type. Letters are dangerous. They live on long after their passions have died.

KYNASTON. They're dangerous only if they're secrets.

VILLIARS. I'd call us a secret, wouldn't you?! There were beginning to be whispers, gossip. The jokes you made in front of the King, that matinee of *The Silent Lady* when Sedley's boys attacked you. "His Duke's Rank Arse"!

KYNASTON. And for that you blame me? Not Sedley?

VILLIARS. I expect Sedley to be vile and stupid. But Sedley's not going anywhere. He's more a fixture now than ever. *(Smiles.)* He's decided to write plays.

KYNASTON. *(On old footing.)* You're joking.

VILLIARS. *(Lisps like Sedley.)* For his woman. *(Pause. They're closer.)*

KYNASTON. "What shall I do to win my lord again?" *(Kynaston reaches out to touch him.)*

VILLIARS. I'm getting married. *(This stops Kynaston. He stares at Villiars.)* It's this Saturday. King's coming. Dryden's composed a sonnet for Peg Hughes to speak. My fiancee is quite a charming thing, really: pretty, rich, surprisingly literate —

KYNASTON. And a woman. What's she like in bed? What's she like to kiss? Does she wear a golden flow as you die in her? Or don't you know?

VILLIARS. *(Explodes.)* I DON'T WANT YOU! *(Calms.)* Not as you are now.

KYNASTON. What do you mean?

VILLIARS. When I did "spend time" with you ... I saw you as a woman. When we were in bed, it was always your bed onstage; I always thought, here I am in a play, inside Desdemona, Cleopatra, poor Ophelia. You're none of them now. And I can't divorce the thought of THEM from what I felt for YOU. I don't know who you are now. I doubt you do.

KYNASTON. I know I'm not twisting my life to fit the way things have become!

VILLIARS. Neither am I! My — *(The bouncer strolls through, eyeing them. Public voice.)* ... My current position on this subject is the logical conclusion of the events as they have occurred. *(The bouncer exits.)* Change your life, Neddy, change what you DO. What we do

is what we are. Take that away and what are we?
KYNASTON.
  "Though he do shake me off,
    Comfort forswear me! Unkindness may do much,
    And his unkindness may defeat my life,
    But never taint my love."
(As he speaks, Kynaston kisses his fingers and lightly lays them on Villiars' cheek. Villiars and the bench and hook go off.)

Scene 4

The stage at the palace. Music plays off. Kynaston has remained onstage. Out of the shadows comes the figure of a large woman. We don't see her face. Kynaston approaches.

KYNASTON. Madam, beg pardon, I'm looking for Miss Nell Gwynn — *(The large woman turns. It's Charles II, dressed as a queen. Heavy make-up.)*
CHARLES. *(Casually.)* You won't find her here.
KYNASTON. *(Shocked, bows.)* ... Majesty?
CHARLES II. King or Queen? Guess quickly!
KYNASTON. Sire —
CHARLES II. Right first time! Do forgive, but we're about to perform one of our palace musicals. *(Hyde enters.)*
HYDE. Majesty? The guests?
CHARLES II. Hyde, we'll need another seat for Mr. — I'm sorry, what is your name? You look familiar.
KYNASTON. Your Majesty, I am Edward Kynaston.
CHARLES II. Kynaston! Mr. Hyde, see our guests are waiting.
HYDE. Yes, Your Majesty. *(Hyde exits.)*
CHARLES II. How in hell did you get in here?
KYNASTON. A former fellow actor is Your Majesty's undercook and has long been dear a friend to me.
CHARLES II. Ah. Well, then, we'll have to execute him. Joke, joke. Calm down. It's the Restoration. No more chop-chop. What you want with Nell? She doesn't like seeing anyone before she goes on. Don't know why you think she'd see you. Nell doesn't like you much.

KYNASTON. Majesty, when she came to audition, my bile was aimed at another. I did not even SEE Miss Gwynn —

CHARLES II. Kynaston. I'm sure you could straighten all this out, but … it's just not important to me.

KYNASTON. *(Explodes.)* IT IS TO ME! *(A high peel of female laughter off. Charles turns to Kynaston. Kynaston and Charles lock eyes as the guests enter. Sedley, Margaret, Lady Meresvale and Miss Frayne enter, chattering away.)*

ALL. *(Ad-lib.)* Here, what's the hold-up! — We've been waiting out there for — ! *(They all stop when they notice Kynaston and the King in their stare-off. Nell pokes her head in from the wings, dressed as Charles II in male garb. She has a mustache.)*

NELL. Charlie, we're at places! What's holding up the — ? *(Stops herself.)*

CHARLES II *(Cold, hard.)* Say what you want.

KYNASTON. I want to act.

CHARLES II. Then act.

KYNASTON. I want to act as I did before.

CHARLES II. You mean the girl parts.

KYNASTON. If you will.

CHARLES II. I won't. You're talking about the Law. My Law. Twenty years ago, it was illegal for a woman to act onstage … in public. But in the palace … women galore! Private musicals, masques, no one gave a damn! Except the clerics. One minister, Mr. Prynne, wrote a pamphlet against all actresses as lewd women and whores. My mother acted in some of those court masques. She felt Mr. Prynne's diatribe was directed at her. So Mr. Prynne was tried, convicted, and sentenced to the stocks where his feet were burned, his ears lopped off, and his tongue cut out. Still, Mr. Prynne never recanted. Some say his stoicism in the face of such "excess" is what fanned the flames of the Puritan revolt. And so off with my father's head, and I to Holland for twenty years. Exile is a dreadful thing for one who knows where is his rightful place. *(Beat.)* I changed the law because it was time for a change; balance the scales, give the girls a chance. If the public rebels, they'll clamor for your return. I shall listen for that clamor, and when that clamor comes, the bells will ring your repeal. But I haven't heard a tinkle yet. Besides, it's a sop to the Church. The priests always preached against boys playing women, said it lead to effeminacy and sodomy. Well, they're priests, they'd know. So we say, "There! See? New Law. No more boys in dresses! Just girls flashing tits! Happy now?"

KYNASTON. Sire. You're wearing a dress.

CHARLES II. *(Pretending to notice.)* Oop. The Emperor has new clothes. Act a man, Kynaston. How hard could it be?

KYNASTON. It's not a question of acting a man; I can act a man; there's no artistry in that. But there are things I can be as a woman I cannot be as a man!

CHARLES II. Such as?

MARGARET. A star. *(All look at Margaret. Nell smiles.)*

NELL. Oh, I think Mr. Kynaston would be a star in any guise. You say there is no artistry in acting a man. Well, then, show us. Let's give Mr. Kynaston the chance to shine as he once gave us.

KYNASTON. *(Not sure what she means.)* ... Miss Gwynn?

NELL. Play a man for us. Show us how well you can act a man ... and perhaps we'll change our minds as to whether you can play a woman. Let's see you as ... Othello. *(Kynaston looks at the assembled guests.)* Take the stage. Please. *(Kynaston positions himself. The others move across the stage from him. He inhales. He performs with elaborate, low voiced bravado.)*

KYNASTON. "It is the cause, it is the cause, my soul. It is the cause — " *(He freezes.)* May I start again?

NELL. *(All condescending charm.)* Yes, of course.

KYNASTON. Thank you. *(He starts again, with even more bravado.)*
"It is the cause, it is the cause, my soul
It is the cause. Yet I'll not shed her blood
Nor scar that whiter skin of hers than snow
And smooth as monumental alabaster:
Yet she must die —
Yet she must — "
(He looks lost.) I'm sorry. Might I — once more?

NELL. *(Smiles.)* Please.

KYNASTON. I'll ... skip ahead a bit. *(He starts to lighten his voice. It becomes airy and tremulous.)*
"Yet she must die, else she'll betray more men.
O, balmy breath, that dost almost persuade
Justice to break her sword! Once more, once more ... "
(Kynaston is shaking now. He begins to weep.) I'm sorry, if I could give it one more go — *(Nell stands, she averts her eyes.)*

NELL. I think we've seen enough.

SEDLEY. *(Sneers.)* Very "delicate" performance.

CHARLES II. *(Clears throat, stands.)* Well now! Show to do. *(Goes up to Kynaston.)* Kynaston? My astronomers tell me that a star's

55

light shines on long after it has died, even though it doesn't know it. I believe you know your way out. Go as you came. *(Turns to Nell.)* Places, sir?

NELL. *(A pained smile.)* Places, madam. *(Charles II and Nell go off backstage. Miss Frayne and Lady Meresvale giggle as Kynaston slowly exits. Margaret watches Kynaston's exit. It looks as if she might cry.)*

SEDLEY. Peggers?

MARGARET. I'm not staying for the performance.

SEDLEY. It is a Royal Command!

MARGARET. Then stay without me.

SEDLEY. But they desire the feminine!

MARGARET. Sir Charles, you bring with you enough femininity to choke a drain! *(Sedley marches off, furious and embarrassed. Margaret looks off where Kynaston exited … but he is gone.)* Oh, Mr. Kynaston … where in the world will you go?

Scene 5

Killigrew's Theater. Backstage. Pepys enters.

PEPYS. June 17, 1662. To the theater to see … well … one has so many choices. There's Mrs. Conley in *Romeo and Juliet* … Mrs. Bracegirdle in *Twelfth Night* … Mrs. Barry in *Hamlet* … and of course, Mrs. Hughes … Mrs. Hughes as Cordelia in *Lear*. *(Margaret enters, in a ragged costume, with a rope around her neck. She has just come offstage to desultory applause. She is angry.)*

MARGARET. Half full house today at best!

PEPYS. Well … summer, you know.

MARGARET. Will you be here for the second performance?

PEPYS. I fear not, Mrs. Hughes.

MARGARET. Going off to see one of my rivals?

PEPYS. Mrs. Hughes, you have no rivals.

MARGARET. Who is it, Mrs. Barry?

PEPYS. … Mrs. Barry, indeed, yes.

MARGARET. I hear she's quite a good Juliet.

PEPYS. And a good Ophelia too! Not that your Ophelia isn't a splendid effort, of course … regardless what the papers said and the

56

audiences …

MARGARET. Mr. Pepys. For whom do you write your diary?

PEPYS. Er … For myself, alone.

MARGARET. Do you enjoy it?

PEPYS. I love it. Don't you love acting?

MARGARET. I think I do. But I cannot do it for myself alone. And truth is I fear, I'm terrible at it. *(She starts to weep.)*

PEPYS. You're too harsh on yourself. You debuted, after all, "The First Actress on the English Stage!"

MARGARET. Mr. Pepys … when I made my debut … was I a good actress?

PEPYS. *(Trying not to lie.)* Mrs. Hughes … there was no comparison.

MARGARET. Mr. Pepys, do you know the whereabouts of Mr. Kynaston?

PEPYS. No, madam. No one does. *(Thomas Killigrew enters. A silky bastard. Mrs. Barry enters behind Killigrew.)*

KILLIGREW. Mrs. Hughes.

MARGARET. *(Surprised to see him.)* Mr. Killigrew!

KILLIGREW. Thought I'd pop in and see the show. Light house today. Do you know Mrs. Barry?

MRS. BARRY. I have heard so much about you, Mrs. Hughes. I wish I could see YOUR Ophelia.

KILLIGREW. Peg, have a cordial with me after the performance. Want to talk about some changes.

MARGARET. *(Has seen the future.)* Of course, Mr. Killigrew. *(Killigrew and Mrs. Barry exit. A stage manager bellows.)*

STAGE MANAGER. Places!

Scene 6

The stage of the CockPit Tavern. Offstage applause. A tatty stage, with orange curtains rolls on. Tiny footlights flicker up. A woman enters onto tiny stage in front of the curtain. She is a hellish M.C. with wild white hair and an eye-patch. She carries a large stick with a suggestive crown at its top. We shall call her Mistress Revels. She bangs the stick for attention.

MISTRESS REVELS. *(Crude cockney.)* AUDIENCE! AUDIENCE! Give me silence now for we needs ears to hear and eyes to see, throats to laugh and hands to clap, for the CockPit Tavern now presents for the fourth time this night that very special Dark Lady of the Sonnets, that Cock-Sure Madam, that Ballsy Bawd, that compleat female stage beauty … Miss Kissy Anytongue! *(Mistress Revels bangs her stick. Applause and whoops from her drunken audience. The curtain parts and Kynaston enters. Kynaston is dressed in a garish gown, huge red wig, white make-up, smeared rouge and lipstick, huge beauty mark. He stands unsteadily. Mistress Revels takes his hand and steadies him. She gives him a "watch yourself, boy-o" look, steps down off the stage and watches from the shadows. Music up. Kynaston clears his throat and begins to sing "No Balls At All.")*
KYNASTON.
Oh, come all ye laddies and listen to me,
And I'll tell you a tale that will fill you with glee;
Of a pretty young maiden so fair and so tall,
Who married a man who had no balls at all!
No balls at all; no balls at all;
She married a man who had no balls at all!
The night of the wedding, she crept into bed;
Her cheeks were so rosy, her ass was so red.
She reached for his penis, his penis was small;
She reached for his balls, but he'd no balls at all!
KYNASTON AND DRUNKS.
No balls at all; no balls at all;
She married a man who had no balls at all!

58

KYNASTON.
>"Oh, mother! Oh, mother! Oh, what shall I do?
>I've married a man who's unable to screw.
>My troubles are many, my pleasures are small,
>For I've married a man who has no balls at all!"

KYNASTON AND DRUNKS.
>No balls at all; no balls at all;
>She married a man who had no balls at all!

(When the song is over, there is applause and cat calls. Mistress revels re-mounts the stage. Kynaston stares out, weaving a bit.)

MISTRESS REVELS. Ere now, that was top-hole! And speaking of HOLE! — it is my understanding, havin' circled the room, as twere, that there are some of you gents — and maybe even some ladies out there — what think our little pretty one ere may not actually be what we call a real, live fish. *(Laughs from crowd.)* Missy dear … Raise the curtain, will you, please? *(Drum roll. Kynaston takes his hands and slowly begins to inch up his dress. Crowd makes a "wooo" sound as the dress goes up and up. Finally, it's high enough to reveal a dark triangle of hair. We realize Kynaston is wearing a Merkin over his crotch. There are cheers from the house. A woman's voice is heard off.)*

WOMAN. *(Off.)* Stop it! STOP IT! *(Mistress Revels turns to look out front. Kynaston squints to see who it is. Crowd silences. Out of the shadows comes a woman in a dark cloak and cowl. She comes onto the stage. She pulls back the cowl. It's Maria.)*

MISTRESS REVELS *(Sneers.)* What you want, Trout?

MARIA. I want the lady. *(The drunk staggers to his feet.)*

MISTRESS REVELS. After we've finished.

MARIA. I'll pay for him. *(Holds up pouch.)* Five pounds. *(Crowd sound: "Oooo." Mistress Revels puts out her hand for the pouch. Maria drops the pouch on the stage. It lands with a clink. Mistress Revels fumes, but she leans over to pick up the pouch. She straightens up and quickly looks inside. Maria goes to Kynaston and takes the stick. She hands it to Mistress Revels. Mistress Revels takes the stick and holds it tight.)*

MISTRESS REVELS. Right then, get the fuck off my stage! *(Maria takes Kynaston's hand and leads him down off the stage. As they make their exit, more "boos" and hisses and whistles. Mistress Revels calls:)* One more time! *(Leads audience.)*

>No balls at all; no balls at all;
>She married a man who had no balls at all!

(Mistress Revels storms off through the curtains.)

Scene 7

A bedchamber at an inn. A simple cot-like bed comes in. A bed table next to it with a wash bowl and cloth. Maria enters with Kynaston. His red wig is gone. He wears a long cape. His make-up is still on. She sets him down on the edge of the bed. He stares out, dull-eyed. Maria lights a candle and puts it on the bedside table. She removes her cloak. She's wearing the Desdemona dress we saw at the top of Act Two. From the table she takes the bowl and cloths.

MARIA. You can stay here for a week. I paid the innkeeper that far. I couldn't take you home. My father wouldn't allow it. Have you eaten?

KYNASTON. *(Dazed rasp.)* ... No.

MARIA. We'll get food and drink. No spirits. Have you slept?

KYNASTON. *(Coughs.)* ... Don't know.

MARIA. Get this off you. *(She begins to remove Kynaston's make-up.)* Took a lot to find you. Landlady said you'd gone weeks ago. No address. Didn't know where to look. Wasn't til I saw a fly-bill for that ... character you were performing.

KYNASTON. Perfectly legal. You saw the evidence betwixt me legs.

MARIA. That went in the sewer ditch first thing.

KYNASTON. *(A wisp of smile.)* You're so ... fastidious. *(Maria stops washing his face. She looks at him a beat. Then she slaps him hard. He recovers. She goes back to washing his face.*

MARIA. If I was fastidious, I wouldn't be here with you, I wouldn't act on the stage. I'd be stitching chastity belts for convent girls. You stink of gin.

KYNASTON. I cook with it. I clean with it. I wash my teeth with it. *(Looks at her.)* Why are you doing this?

MARIA. What, removing the grime and filth from you? 'Cause I won't let you dirty the sheets. *(Maria removes the cape. Kynaston is naked but for an undergarment. There are lots of scars and bruises from his attack. Touches his chest.)* Hurt when I touch this?

KYNASTON. I don't feel ANYTHING when you touch whatever you're touching. *(Maria goes back to washing him. Kynaston comes back to life a bit, still woozy, but articulate.)* So you live with your father, eh? Must be a strict sort. I mean, if he won't let you bring home gin-soaked bum boys who wear false twats, he mustn't be very open minded.

MARIA.   My father was an actor, before Cromwell. He's retired from the stage. Binds books now. He would welcome you, gin and all, but he'd give you the stable, and I think you need a dry room for a good few nights.

KYNASTON.   Your father sounds like heaven. Maybe I should marry him. I said I'd never wed an actor, but a book-binder I could manage. What's his name?

MARIA.   George.

KYNASTON.   Oh. I've had a George. No fun. They marry duchesses at the earliest convenience. Betterton told me you were a good actress. Said you had an "effective lack of affectation." The great sin of all actors: alliteration. We treat every sentence as a test of our diction. Clicking away, teeth and lips and tongues. Good practice for all sorts of things, theater-related and not. *(Winces.)* That's starting to hurt a bit.

MARIA.   *(Wipes more gently.)* Sorry. *(Moves from the bed, her back to him.)* I shall stay here with you tonight. *(Kynaston looks at Maria. She wrings out the cloth into the bowl.)*

KYNASTON.   You want to make sure I don't run off? *(Maria stands with the bowl and cloth. She turns to him.)*

MARIA.   ... No. *(They look at each other.)*

KYNASTON.   I have never slept with a woman. Except myself. *(Maria sets down the bowl and cloth. She takes off her Desdemona gown. She wears a shift, like the doll Betterton used. She sits next to Kynaston on the bed.)*

MARIA.   Tell me what men do.

KYNASTON.   With women?

MARIA.   With men.

KYNASTON.   They ... we ... Well, it depends. With men and women, there's a "man," and there's a "woman." Well ... sometimes, on occasion, it's the same with men and men.

MARIA.   Were you the man or the woman? *(Kynaston gives her a look.)* That means?

KYNASTON.   Would you like me to show you? *(Maria nods. Kynaston rises. He indicates that Maria stand. She does. Kynaston lies down on the bed, face down. he looks up at her. He indicates that she "mount" him from behind.)* Right, in the saddle. *(Tentatively, Maria does so. She "rides" his haunches.)*

MARIA. I see. And am I the man now or the woman?

KYNASTON. You're the man.

MARIA. And you're the woman.

KYNASTON. Yes.

MARIA. Isn't much to do.

KYNASTON. Not with what we're given.

MARIA. What's it like the other way? *(Kynaston indicates that Maria hop off. She does. Kynaston indicates that she lie down, face forward. Maria does so. Then Kynaston comes behind her and lies gently on top of her.)* So … who am I now?

KYNASTON. You're the woman.

MARIA. And you're — ?

KYNASTON. I'm the man. Or so I assume. I've never been up here before. Quite a view.

MARIA. But I'm the man-woman.

KYNASTON. Yes, you're the man-woman. Or the woman-woman. It works both ways. *(Maria turns over so that she is now on her back looking up at Kynaston above her.)*

MARIA. And what am I now?

KYNASTON. The woman.

MARIA. Still?

KYNASTON. Yes. *(Maria puts one leg around his back and slowly, slowly revolves him until he's lying with his back on the bed and she is above him.)*

MARIA. And now what am I?

KYNASTON. The woman. *(Maria puts her arms around him.)*

MARIA. And now?

KYNASTON. The woman.

MARIA. And you are —

KYNASTON. The man. *(Maria rises and pulls Kynaston up so that he's kneeling on the bed, facing her.)*

MARIA. And now? Who are you now?

KYNASTON. I don't know. *(Silence. Maria comes forward to kiss Kynaston on his chest, where the bruises and scars are.)*

MARIA. *(Kissing.)* Can you feel that?

KYNASTON. No.

MARIA. *(Kissing.)* That?

KYNASTON. *(Closes eyes.)* No.

MARIA. *(Kissing.)* That?

KYNASTON. *(Eyes closed.)* … Yes. It hurts … *(Maria stops kissing him. She puts her arms around his torso. She looks up at him. He looks at her. He looks at her. He may kiss her. Finally:)* Wait. Before we do … Tell me something.

MARIA. *(Eyes closed.)* Anything.

KYNASTON. How do you die?

MARIA. Die?

KYNASTON. As Desdemona. How do you die? *(Maria opens her eyes and stares at him. Then she pulls her shift back up. She sits on the side of the bed, away from him. She starts to cry.)* I'm sorry, I should not have asked, I — I'm — I really shouldn't —

MARIA. *(Bitter, through tears.)* I fight him!

KYNASTON. Excuse me?

MARIA. I fight him off, I fight for my life! I won't let him kill me! But he still kills me! I always hated you as Desdemona! You never fought! You just died "beautifully"! No woman would die like that, no matter how much she loved him! A woman would fight! She'd fight and leave her love, if that were it! Only a man would act it any other way! *(Maria gathers her things, her cloak, etc. And rushes to the door. She stops, her hand on the knob. She does not turn to Kynaston.)* You can stay here the week. I've paid. *(She exits. Door slam. The candle near the bed goes out. Lights go out.)*

Scene 8

The same room. Gray daylight. Kynaston asleep in the bed-clothes. A loud knocking off. Male voice:

VOICE. Edward Kynaston! Edward Kynaston within! *(Kynaston stirs. The door swings open violently. Kynaston sits up. A thug enters, all in black. He looks very threatening.)*

THUG. Kynaston. Get up. Put clothes on.

KYNASTON. *(Dazed, scared.)* … I … don't have my clothes. *(Thug takes off his own black cape and tosses it at Kynaston.)*

THUG. Put this round. *(Kynaston wraps the cape around himself. The thug turns and calls out through the door.)* He's clad. Decent as will. *(Nell Gwynn enters. She is dressed in expensive but subdued travel clothes. She gives the thug a baleful glance.)*

NELL. Shit, wouldn't want to see him without the drapery. Scorch my fuckin' eyes.

KYNASTON. *(Squints.)* Miss Gwynn?

NELL. Innkeep says you've been up here best of a week. Where'd you get money for that, I wonder, especially as you look such a rat tail. Wait outside. *(Thug exits.)*

KYNASTON. What do you want?

NELL. *(Looks down.)* ... To apologize. For what I did to you at the palace. I was warranted in my anger but had no right to vent it in that way. You blocked my way, Ned. You stopped me from seeing Mr. Betterton.

KYNASTON. My refusal was not aimed at you but at the Hughes.

NELL. That supposed to make me feel better? "Oh, I wasn't out to ruin YOUR life, it was some OTHER woman." Peg's my friend.

KYNASTON. No professional jealousy?

NELL. We play different kinds of parts. She's the tragic type. Me, I do comedies.

KYNASTON. And she's no rival for the King's affections?

NELL. *(Looks away.)* ... Not she. Charlie's got a new tart. French. Catholic, too. Clerics've been protesting outside the palace all week. Other day, they stopped my carriage, thought I was her. I yelled: "You got the wrong coach! I'm the PROTESTANT whore!" Charlie's been decent though. Set me up a house, monies, lands, jewels. I'm still faithful to him.

KYNASTON. You mean, in your "way."

NELL. *(Hard.)* No. I'm faithful in the way the word faithful means. *(Beat.)* I'm gonna work for Mr. Betterton. Had offers from the others, but he's had rum luck and could use a boost.

KYNASTON. Why rum luck?

NELL. He lost his Desdemona, Maria whatzit. Up and quit the other day.

KYNASTON. What happened?

NELL. She said she'd ne'er assay the role again after some discussion she had with you about her "death scene." Problem is Betterton had scheduled *Othello* for tonight. Charlie's coming, everybody's in tow. The Crown wants to decide if it should patronize Mr. Betterton's theater again, so there's a lot riding. Then this Maria Nobody pops off, and Mr. B's without his Mrs. O.

KYNASTON. What about you?

NELL. Please. Who wants to see a FUNNY Desdemona? He got Peg. "The Hughes."

KYNASTON. I thought she worked for Killigrew.

64

NELL. He fired her.

KYNASTON. Why?

NELL. She's no good. I say this as a friend.

KYNASTON. But she was a star …

NELL. Look. I was an orange girl. I sold fruit. Some fruit people paid dear for! Why? 'Cause they was rare. When Peg hit the stage she was rare. Now: We've got fruit all over town! Mrs. Orange, Mrs. Peach, bloody Mrs. Pomegranate! Peg's like the first soldier over the barricades: a big cheer and then … bang! She's a mess now. When she heard the King and all were coming tonight, she refused to go on. But Sedley has put money in Betterton's theater now. He insists it is Peg or none. So there's no option.

KYNASTON. *(Suspicious.)* What do you want?

NELL. Help her.

KYNASTON. "Help…?"

NELL. If you took her in hand … and taught her some tricks, some turns … I think she could get the courage to go on!

KYNASTON. *(Disbelief, it's laughable.)* No!

NELL. There's money in my purse.

KYNASTON. NO!!! Teach the woman who drove me from the stage to help the man who fired me from his theater to entertain the King who outlawed me from life?!!!

NELL. You ever see her onstage?

KYNASTON. No.

NELL. You should have.

KYNASTON. Why, what's she like?

NELL. You. She does you. Every inflection, every bat of the eye. Bits of business, vocal tricks. Like an engraving.

KYNASTON. Then she shouldn't be half bad.

NELL. It don't work. I do mimicry, Ned. I can mimic anyone. Woman, man. I did Charlie so well once, I almost got the Spanish ambassador to think England wanted to give Scotland to Portugal. I can mimic the Queen herself … but it don't "fit."

KYNASTON. We are not always what we do.

NELL. Say that. I could be made Countess of Cleveland, I'm still a bejeweled fish. *(Pause.)* Most of the play she'd be fine. It's the end what's bad. When she dies.

KYNASTON. The murder.

NELL. She's only played it once. That first time. Never since.

KYNASTON. What about the night you and the King were going to go —

NELL. She didn't play that night. Because of what happened to you in the park.

KYNASTON. Because her lover had me beaten.

NELL. That's him, not her. Cut the woman from the man.

KYNASTON. I have been trying.

NELL. *(After a beat.)* I can offer you more than money. I can offer you a friend.

KYNASTON. Friends I have had. Give me an audience.

NELL. If that's what you want, you must take it with your own hands. A man isn't how he walks or how he speaks, it's what he DOES.

KYNASTON. And what does a man do? According to their onstage characters, they covet riches and power. They are slaves to lust and fear. They plot revenge, murder and then die. Can I be such a man? *(Muses darkly.)* Take it with my own hands. *(Kynaston has made up his mind.)* You have clothes?

NELL. *(Calls.)* Olly! *(The thug reenters.)* Olly, give Mr. Kynaston your clothes. *(The thug frowns.)* C'mon, Olly, be a gent. Let's see what makes you swagger so! *(Nell smiles at the thug. Grudgingly, he starts to remove his pants.)*

Scene 9

The stage at Duke's Theater. The bed is set. Betterton and Sedley pace before it. Betterton wears his Othello *cloak. Sedley's outfit is outrageous as always. Sedley stops and snaps his fingers. He's got an idea.*

SEDLEY. Perhaps —

BETTERTON. *(Turns.)* What.

SEDLEY. What if she played it as a no-dialogue part? No voice?

BETTERTON. Meaning?

SEDLEY. *(Making it up as he goes.)*
  "More poignant for her silenced flute,
    This evening's Desdemona's mute!"

BETTERTON. *(Stares at this idiot.)* Oh, lord … and I'm producing your first play.

66

SEDLEY. Well, then, what shall we do? Cancel the performance?
BETTERTON. Cancel the play because one of the actors is no good? Start doing that, there won't be a show left on the planet! *(Nell enters. Betterton and Sedley turn to see her.)*
NELL. Gentlemen, I have procured Peg a tutor. *(Kynaston enters. A beat as they all stop and stare at each other.)*
BETTERTON. *(A weak smile.)* Ned.
KYNASTON. *(Wary.)* Tommy. Sedley.
SEDLEY. *(Harrumphing.)* Some rules of engagement, Kynaston —
KYNASTON. *(Cuts him off.)* First rule: You're out. Off the stage.
SEDLEY. *(Protesting.)* Betterton — !
BETTERTON. Best work in private, Sir Charles. We've less than half an hour.
SEDLEY. *(Fumes.)* We shall exeunt, Kynaston, but mark our history and my property. You are assisting MY Desdemona, as all the city know. Don't try anything funny — give her a funny voice or a funny walk, a squint. I'll notice. And I won't like it! *(Sedley huffs and exits.)*
BETTERTON. Neddy, I can't thank you e—
KYNASTON. Then don't.
BETTERTON. ... I've tried everything with her, every trick. The girl's a wash-out. If you can just make her passable. What do you need? Wine? Some cheese?
KYNASTON. A share.
BETTERTON. ... I would say, "What?" but you will say —
KYNASTON. "A share."
BETTERTON. How big?
KYNASTON. Five. Partner?
BETTERTON. Thief! Shall I bring her in?
KYNASTON. *(Nods.)* Would you be a dear?
BETTERTON. At once, Mr. Kynaston ... *(Sotto voce.)* ... you arrogant bung-house shit. *(Betterton exits.)*
NELL. I'd best go, too. See you after! *(Nell exits. Kynaston puts on the cloak. He looks at the bed. He adjusts the sheets. He fluffs the curtains. He picks up a white pillow. Maria enters. He turns to see her.)*
KYNASTON. *(Surprised.)* I thought you'd quit.
MARIA. *(Cool.)* I quit the role of Desdemona. I play Emilia now. My father advised the long view: "Desdemonas shine 'twixt the ages of sixteen and twenty-five, but Emilias go on forever." Still doing the seamstress work.
KYNASTON. That's not my pillow.

MARIA. Different one. It's for Mrs. Hughes.

KYNASTON. *(Takes it.)* Yes, mine was red. And you sewed pearls in it, as I recall … although from the seats you couldn't see them.

MARIA. *(Softens.)* The pearls were for you.

KYNASTON. I am sorry about the night in the inn. I had been trying to act a man, but hadn't found the role.

MARIA. We are never suited for the roles we most desire. *(Gives him a hard look.)* Why'd you come back to do this?

KYNASTON. *(Jaunty and theatrical.)* "The stage beckoned and I picked up my cue." *(Terse.)* Work to be done. I'm told men live for their work. And I have lived for this chance.

MARIA. To do what?

KYNASTON. *(Mysterious.)* … You shall see. *(Margaret enters. She wears a sparkling Desdemona gown. Kynaston turns to see her. He tosses down the pillow.)*

MARGARET. *(Cool.)* Mr. Kynaston.

KYNASTON. *(Cool.)* Mrs. Hughes. Welcome to my bedchamber. *(Kynaston looks at Maria. Maria exits.)*

MARGARET. I am given to understand you intend — *(Kynaston starts to move, all business.)*

KYNASTON. Let's get to work, shall we? *(Re: gown.)* You wearing that tonight?

MARGARET. … Yes.

KYNASTON. Lose it.

MARGARET. Sir Charles designed this costume especially.

KYNASTON. It looks it. Strip down to your shift.

MARGARET. Strip — ! Here now, if you think you can teach me how to be a woman — !

KYNASTON. I'm not teaching you how to be a WOMAN! I'm teaching you how to be DESDEMONA!

MARGARET. I DON'T WANT TO BE DESDEMONA!!! I DON'T WANT TO ACT EVER AGAIN!!! *(Starts off, weeping.)* I am done with the stage — !

KYNASTON. *(Grabbing her.)* NO! YOU CLAIMED THE ROLE, NOW HOLD ONTO IT TIL THEY PRY YOUR FINGERS FROM ITS NECK! MORE THAN THE ROLE, YOU HOLD THIS THEATER IN YOUR HAND! SO STAND STILL, DRY YOUR EYES, AND STRIP! *(Margaret shimmies out of her gown.)*

KYNASTON. Muss the hair before the scene. Not like that. That's puffing to make it look attractive when it's merely arranged. Roll on a sheet, make it real. Flat on one side would be good. And no blush on your cheeks. No lip paint. White cheeks, pale lips. Blood drains down at sleep, not up to the face.

MARGARET. I know you consider this "your" part —

KYNASTON. No. It's your part. And frankly, it's not that "good" a part. Most of Shakespeare's women aren't very good parts, except the crazy ones. Couple of scenes, then off they go. Even their death scenes aren't very good. No great speeches for the girls. What's Desdemona's last line. "Farewell." What's that?

MARGARET. YOU played that line with a whisper and a cough.

KYNASTON. Shit with sugar on it. The way Betterton does the last scene, there are 32 lines, cutting 17. You start on the bed. Go. *(Margaret drapes herself on the bed.)* Not like that. That's like me.

MARGARET. *(Sits up.)* Well, then, how should I do it?

KYNASTON. How do you get into BED? C'mon, woman, how'd you get this PART? *(Margaret fumes. She flops down on the bed and pulls the duvet over her.)* It's Cyprus in summer. *(Margaret flings off the duvet. She flips over on her back.)* Is that how you sleep?

MARGARET. *(Sits up again.)* How am I supposed to know how I sleep? I'm SLEEPING while I sleep!

KYNASTON. What do your lovers tell you? *(Beat. Margaret turns over on her stomach and curls up in a fetal position.)* Good, curled up in ball, spread over both sides of the bed. Sounds right to me. Right! First line!

MARGARET. *(Sits up.)* "Who's there? Othello?"

KYNASTON. Why's she say that? "Who's there? Othello?" She think it's not really him? No. She knows it's him, she's just not AWAKE yet.

MARGARET. Yes, I see.

KYNASTON. So lie back down. Stay down for four lines. She won't really be awake until she says: "Alas, my lord, what may you mean by that?" Onward.

MARGARET. *(Lies down; sleep sound.)* "Will you come to bed, my lord?"

KYNASTON. "Have you pray'd tonight, Desdemona?"

MARGARET. *(Yawns.)* "Ay, my lord."

KYNASTON.
   "If you bethink yourself of any crime
    Unreconciled as yet to heaven and grace,
    Solicit for it straight."

MARGARET. *(Sits up; alert.)* "Alas, my lord, what may you mean by that?"

KYNASTON.
   "Well, do it, and be brief; I will walk by:
      I would not kill thy unprepared spirit;
      No; heaven forfend! I would not kill thy soul."
   There'll be thunder there.
MARGARET. *(Rises, smiles uncertainly.)* "Talk you of killing?"
KYNASTON. Why are you smiling?
MARGARET. YOU always — I think he's joking.
KYNASTON. Othello's funny? Plays jokes on you a lot, does he?
MARGARET. No, but —
KYNASTON. Then don't act with what isn't there! The man's
been a festering boil for three fucking hours, hasn't he?
MARGARET. Yes.
KYNASTON. And now he's come to your bedroom, woke you
up, and told you pray before you die!
MARGARET. Yes.
KYNASTON. So what's the line?
MARGARET. *(Shocked, stands.)* "Talk you of killing!"
KYNASTON. Keep going. *(Othello voice.)* "Ay, I do."
MARGARET. *(Crosses herself.)* "Then heaven have mercy on me."
KYNASTON. Good, keep that. "Think on thy sins."
MARGARET. "They are loves I bear to you."
KYNASTON. "Ay, and for that thou diest."
MARGARET. *(Backs away oddly.)* "That death's unnatural that
kills for loving!" *(Kynaston does not move.)*
KYNASTON. "Peace and be still!" And I MEAN that!
MARGARET. But Othello is advancing on her.
KYNASTON. AM I? DO YOU SEE ME MOVING?
MARGARET. Well, no —
KYNASTON. *(A shout.)* Take one step back on "That death's
unnatural," then a stumble after "that kills for loving."
MARGARET. I don't know if I can remember the stumble—
KYNASTON. You will. *(Very loud.)* "Ay, and for that thou diest!"
MARGARET. "That death's unnatural *(Steps back one step.)* that
kills for loving!"
KYNASTON. *(Bellows.)* "PEACE AND BE STILL!!!" *(Margaret
almost falls.)*
MARGARET. "I will so. What's the matter?"
KYNASTON. "That handkerchief which I so loved and gave thee
Thou gavest to Cassio."
MARGARET. "No, by my life and soul!

70

Send for the man and ask him."

KYNASTON. *(Sarcastic.)* … "Send for the man"? "Send for the man"? That's easy to say, isn't it? "Send for the man." Cassio's name gives her the willies.

MARGARET. But she doesn't say the name "Cassio."

KYNASTON. Ah-ha!

MARGARET. I'm lost.

KYNASTON. You think Iago plucked Cassio out of nowhere? If Iago was going to poison the Moor's mind with a fictive lover for Desdemona, he had to pick someone who made sense. It couldn't be Jo-Jo, the Mute Boy. Iago picked Cassio because in truth Desdemona DOES fancy him! Had not she loved the Moor, she might have loved good Cassio. So when Othello mentions him, yes, she must say "Call for Cassio," but his name does not come easy.

MARGARET. But she doesn't SAY his name!

KYNASTON. *(Luring her into the idea.)* Yes…?

MARGARET. *(Gets the point.)* Oh.

KYNASTON. *(Othello voice.)*
   "That handkerchief which I so loved and gave thee
      Thou gavest to Cassio."

MARGARET. *(Confused.)*
   "No, by my life and soul!
      Send for C … the man and ask him."

KYNASTON. *(Smiles.)* Good girl! Right, now, this next exchange of seven lines comes fast!

MARGARET. Why?

KYNASTON. Because everyone always does them slow. Very deliberate, very stately. "Ooo, look at him 'advance' on her." We want to get to the murder faster than they expect.

MARGARET. How can you say things like "While I say one prayer" fast?

KYNASTON. You're not in charge of this part of the scene, the Moor is. The Moor does his lines fast, it's your job to slap your words in fast as you can or else the Moor will run you down and kill you six lines sooner!
   "His mouth is stopped;
      Honest Iago hath ta'en order for 't! GO!"

MARGARET. *(Fast.)* "O, my fear interprets! What he is dead?"

KYNASTON. *(Faster.)*
   "Had all his hairs been lives, my great revenge
      Had stomach for them all."

71

MARGARET. *(Faster.)* "Alas, he is betray'd, and I undone!"

KYNASTON. *(Faster still.)* "Out, strumpet! Weep'st thou for him to my face?"

MARGARET. *(Tripping over lines.)* "O, banish me, my lord, but kill me not!"

KYNASTON. *(Overlaps her.)* "Down, strumpet!"

MARGARET. *(Falls back on bed.)* "Kill me to-morrow; let me live tonight!"

KYNASTON. "Nay, if you strive — "

MARGARET. *(Overlaps "if you strive.")* "But half an hour!"

KYNASTON. "Being done, there is no pause."

MARGARET. *(On her knees.)* "But while I say one prayer!"

KYNASTON. *(Grabs up pillow.)* "It is too late."

MARGARET. *(Shrieks.)* AHHHH! *(They freeze in a pose, he above her, her hands in front of her to protect her.)*

KYNASTON. And there'll be thunder there as well. *(Kynaston tosses down the pillow. Sound: noise of audience entering off.)* See what comes out of a rehearsal?

MARGARET. I had planned to scream anyway.

KYNASTON. Good for you.

MARGARET. Now do it.

KYNASTON. What.

MARGARET. Throw me on the bed. Kill me.

KYNASTON. No.

MARGARET. We start the play in fifteen minutes. We've got to finish this off.

KYNASTON. Save something for the moment. Always do something different than you planned. Good to throw yourself off a bit. Recall what we've done to this point in the scene. Then when you die … surprise me. Tommy!

MARGARET. But how do I know Mr. Betterton will do as you have done?

KYNASTON. You don't. Because he won't. *(Betterton and Sedley enter.)*

BETTERTON. All ready to go?

KYNASTON. Yes. I'm playing the Moor.

BETTERTON. Pardon?

KYNASTON. Mrs. Hughes insists. *(Pause. Betterton and Sedley turn to her.)*

BETTERTON. Mrs. Hughes —

MARGARET. I do.

SEDLEY. Does he even know the part?

BETTERTON. *(Glowers at Kynaston.)* Oh, yes. He knows it.

SEDLEY. This is an outrage!

KYNASTON. Wait'll you see us do *Macbeth*!

BETTERTON. *(Staggers back.)* AHHH! *(Betterton rushes off.)*

KYNASTON. Now, quickly, someone get me boot black.

MARGARET. Boot black?

KYNASTON. Othello's still a moor, yes?

SEDLEY. I have boot black!

KYNASTON. WITH you?

SEDLEY. A scuff, sir, is a dreadful thing. *(Hands it over.)*

KYNASTON. Sedley, you are useful after all. Now, clear off!

SEDLEY. Yes, yes, the stage, sir, is yours! *(Sedley exits.)*

MARGARET. Mr. Kynaston. My thanks.

KYNASTON. It's not a good role, Desdemona. Go for Lavinia. Or Cleopatra.

MARGARET. Why they?

KYNASTON. Because when Lavinia loses her tongue and hands … she still must assert herself.

MARGARET. And Cleopatra?

KYNASTON. She kills herself with the sting of an asp. A snake to her breast, that men had kissed and a child would suckle. "Those who do die, Do never recover." *(Kynaston holds the pillow and fixes her with a dead stare.)* I blame you for my death.

MARGARET. What's that from?

KYNASTON. Nothing. *(Beat.)* See you onstage. *(Margaret exits. Kynaston begins to dress and make up as Othello.)*

  "It is the cause, it is the cause, my soul.
   Let me not name it to you, you chaste stars!
   It is the cause. Yet I'll not shed her blood,
   Nor scar the whiter skin of hers than snow,
   And smooth as monumental alabaster.
   Yet she must die, else she'll betray more men.
   Put out the light, and then put out the light.
   If I quench thee, thou flaming minister,
   I can again thy former light restore."
(Loud thunder. Lights change.)

Scene 10

Lights come back up almost immediately. Onstage at the Duke's Theater. A large bed with flowing curtains. No other furniture. Figure lies on the bed. Kynaston enters. Another rumble of thunder. The scene is played as they rehearsed it.

MARGARET. "Who's there? Othello?"

KYNASTON. "Ay, Desdemona."

MARGARET. "Will you come to bed, my lord?"

KYNASTON. "Have you pray'd tonight, Desdemona?"

MARGARET. "Ay, my lord."

KYNASTON.
"If you bethink yourself of any crime
    Unreconciled as yet to heaven and grace,
    Solicit for it straight."

MARGARET. "Alas, my lord, what may you mean by that?"

KYNASTON.
"Well, do it, and be brief; I will walk by:
    I would not kill thy unprepared spirit;
    No; heaven forfend! I would not kill thy soul."

(Thunder. Margaret rises.)

MARGARET. "Talk you of killing?"

KYNASTON. "Ay, I do."

MARGARET. "Then heaven have mercy on me."

KYNASTON. "Think on thy sins."

MARGARET. "They are loves I bear to you."

KYNASTON. "Ay, and for that thou diest."

MARGARET. "That death's unnatural that kills for loving!"

KYNASTON. "Peace and be still!'

MARGARET. "I will so. What's the matter?"

KYNASTON.
"That handkerchief which I so loved and gave thee
    Thou gavest to Cassio."

MARGARET.
"No, by my life and soul!
    Send for C … the man and ask him."

KYNASTON.

"His mouth is stopped.

Honest Iago hath ta'en order for 't."

(Rumble of thunder.)

MARGARET. "O, my fear interprets! What he is dead?"

KYNASTON.

"Had all his hairs been lives, my great revenge

Had stomach for them all."

MARGARET. "Alas, he is betray'd, and I undone!"

KYNASTON. "Out, strumpet! Weep'st thou for him to my face?"

MARGARET. "O, banish me, my lord, but kill me not!"

KYNASTON. "Down, strumpet!"

MARGARET. "Kill me to-morrow; let me live tonight!"

KYNASTON. "Nay, if you strive, — "

MARGARET. "But half an hour!"

KYNASTON. "Being done, there is no pause."

MARGARET. "But while I say one prayer!"

KYNASTON. "It is too late."

MARGARET. AHHHHH! *(Wild thunder during what follows next: Kynaston grabs up the pillow and stares down at Margaret a beat. Then Kynaston thrusts Margaret on the bed and smothers her. She struggles. He is pressing hard. She starts to flail arms and legs. He won't let up. She screams from underneath the pillow. Knocking at door. Kynaston and Margaret struggle. She claws at his face. She slaps his arms. She slides from under him and collapses on the floor, choking. To the audience.)* HELP! HELP ME! HE'S KILL — ! *(Kynaston lunges at her and smothers her on the floor, not the bed. "OHHH!" from the crowd. Beat. Knocks off.)*

MARIA. *(Off.)* "My lord, my lord! What ho! My lord, my lord!"

KYNASTON. *(Still smothering.)*

"What noise is this? Not dead? Not quite yet dead?

I that am cruel am yet merciful;

I would not have thee linger in thy pain:

So, so."

(Maria dressed as Emilia, enters.)

MARIA. "My lord — " *(Kynaston stares off. A glassy stare. Maria leans down to the floor. She listens at Margaret's heart. Kynaston stands above, looking lost. Maria looks back up at Kynaston, her eyes wide. Maria stands and looks offstage and opens her mouth to speak. Then Margaret's hand moves.)*

MARGARET. *(Weak voiced.)* "O, falsely, falsely murdered."

MARIA. *(Surprised.)*

"A ... las, what cry is that?
O, sweet mistress, speak!
Who hath done this deed?"
MARGARET.
"Nobody. I myself. Farewell:
Commend me to my kind lord:
O, farewell."
(Margaret "Dies." Maria looks up at Kynaston and sighs relief.)
KYNASTON. "Why, how should she be murdered?" *(Winks at her. Maria smiles and opens her mouth to speak when:)*
AUDIENCE MEMBER. BRAVA!
MARIA. "Alas, who knows — " *(More audience members: "BRAVO! BRAVA! HUGHES! HUGHES!" Cheers and stamping. Kynaston turns and leans down to Margaret, a hand outstretched. Margaret sits up. She eyes Kynaston. He extends his hand. She takes it. Kynaston pulls Margaret to her feet. Finally Kynaston quiets the house. Silence. Then Kynaston turns to Margaret and indicates that she must speak. Margaret looks at Kynaston a beat. Then she turns out front.)*
MARGARET. Please. We still have one more scene. *(Margaret grins and curtsies. Applause. Kynaston smiles at her. Margaret smiles back at Kynaston. Maria backs away. The applause dies. Kynaston picks up his red pillow. He treats it as a dying lover.)*
KYNASTON.
"Here is my journey's end.
Desdemona's dead.
I kissed thee ere I killed thee.
No way but this.
Killing myself
To die upon a kiss."
(Kynaston kisses the pillow goodbye. He lays it down on the bed. Then he slowly eases himself down onto it. Applause and cheers. The lights show that the curtain has lowered.)

Scene 11

Backstage after the show. Kynaston, Margaret, and Maria have not moved. Suddenly the stage is filled with people. Pepys, Sedley, Betterton, and Nell are the first in from stage right. Margaret sits up as they rush in, their words practically falling over each other.

PEPYS. Huzzahs, Mrs. Hughes! Amazing!

SEDLEY. My dear, I knew you could do it!

BETTERTON. Fantastic, madam, top to bottom!

NELL. When Ned came at you like that, I almost got up there meself and kicked 'im in the nuts! *(Margaret is all smiles and about to speak when suddenly king Charles II, Villiars, Lady Meresvale, and Miss Frayne enter from stage left.)*

CHARLES II. Mrs. Hughes.

MARGARET. Majesty…?

CHARLES II. Brava, madam, good show, thrills and chills, all the way around.

MARGARET. Thank you, Your Majesty!

CHARLES II. Very different, Betterton. That new ending was very real. Almost too much so. But restorative somehow. Well, that's tragedy for you: Awe and terror and yet we still go to dinner. *(To the women.)* Ladies? *(Charles II, Lady Meresvale, and Miss Frayne turn and exit off left. Nell turns away, hurt by Charles II. Villiars remains a beat and looks at Kynaston.)*

VILLIARS. Bravo. *(Villiars exits. Sedley becomes the expansive host.)*

SEDLEY. Well, then! Dinner indeed! Chesterfield's? My treat!

PEPYS. I'll take you up on that!

SEDLEY. *(To Nell.)* Miss Gwynn, lost in thought?

NELL. Just thinking what I'd give to see Ned play Rosalind again. But not now. Now Rosalind's MY PART! *(Nell exits with Pepys and Sedley.)*

BETTERTON. You know … doing *As You Like It* next week … could use a good Jacques.

KYNASTON. Possibly.

BETTERTON. You'll know best what suits. Well! Rehearsal in the morning! Chance to get it right again, eh? *(Betterton exits. Margaret looks at Kynaston.)*

MARGARET. You almost killed me.

KYNASTON. I did kill you, you just didn't die.

MARGARET. I felt you pressing on me, and then I felt you pull away. What stopped you from finishing me off?

KYNASTON. I surprised myself. I finally got the death scene right. *(Beat.)* See you in the morning at rehearsal. *(Margaret smiles. She exits. Pepys comes onstage and faces down front.)*

PEPYS.
> 'Tis said a fit play,
> Does not need an epilogue.
> But if a play has an epilogue,
> Might as well it be a fitting one.

(The company comes downstage from the darkness.)
> And so our Ned has come his travels,
> Twirled and twisted, all unravels.
> Comes now the age where he must brave
> A world in which he need not shave.

CHARLES II.
> For he who knows which laws to flex
> Can take his joy from either sex.

BETTERTON.
> Ned works, in fact,
> And plys his wares.
> For he that acts
> Will own five shares.

NELL.
> Never Hamlet,
> Never Lear,
> He would play other fellows
> Jacques, Kent, and Chanticleer,
> But nevermore Othellos.

MARGARET.
> And when he left the boards he ran
> To home and hearth like any man.

MARIA.
> And there did fashion a new life
> Where cares and joys and normal strife
> Distract from all that he forsook:

SEDLEY.
> The knights and knaves …

VILLIARS.
> And errant dukes.

KYNASTON.
> What does it matter,
> What he lost?
> That world was gone,
> And Tempest toss'd
> He found himself upon a shore
> Where he could act
> And asked no more.

PEPYS. "To the theater to see the actor Kynaston. He had good fortune to appear in many guises, and by the end was surely the handsomest man in the house." *(Kynaston still holds the pillow from the murder scene. He brings it up to his face. He breathes in its scent. He closes his eyes and smiles. He exhales. Lights fade.)*

End of Play

PROPERTY LIST

Diary, pen (PEPYS)
Red pillow (BETTERTON, MARIA, MARGARET, KYNASTON)
Wig (KYNASTON, VILLIARS)
Makeup removing kit (BETTERTON, KYNASTON)
Letter (MARIA, KYNASTON)
Gold stick with red silk tassel, yellow gloves (SEDLEY)
Lantern (MARIA)
Flyer (VILLIARS)
Gold helmet, gold sword and shield (NELL)
Glove (KYNASTON)
Burlap bags of excrement (AUDIENCE)
Cloth (MARIA)
Handkerchief (KYNASTON)
Letter (MARIA, KYNASTON)
State papers (CHARLES II)
Cudgels, sticks (RUFFIANS)
Fans (LADIES)
Coffee (PEPYS, KYNASTON)
Cane, sunglasses, white apron (KYNASTON)
Life-size doll (BETTERTON)
Rope (MARGARET)
Suggestive stick (MISTRESS REVELS)
Merkin (KYNASTON)
Pouch with coins (MARIA)
Candle, match, bowl, cloths, water (MARIA)
White pillow (MARGARET, KYNASTON)

SOUND EFFECTS

3 knocks of a cane
Stage thunder
Applause
Laughter
Cheers
Whistle
Seven bells
Drum roll
Knock on door
Music
Steam hissing
Sound of audience entering
Cheers and feet stomping

NEW PLAYS

★ **GUARDIANS by Peter Morris.** In this unflinching look at war, a disgraced American soldier discloses the truth about Abu Ghraib prison, and a clever English journalist reveals how he faked a similar story for the London tabloids. "Compelling, sympathetic and powerful." *–NY Times.* "Sends you into a state of moral turbulence." *–Sunday Times (UK).* "Nothing short of remarkable." *–Village Voice.* [1M, 1W] ISBN: 978-0-8222-2177-7

★ **BLUE DOOR by Tanya Barfield.** Three generations of men (all played by one actor), from slavery through Black Power, challenge Lewis, a tenured professor of mathematics, to embark on a journey combining past and present. "A teasing flare for words." *–Village Voice.* "Unfailingly thought-provoking." *–LA Times.* "The play moves with the speed and logic of a dream." *–Seattle Weekly.* [2M] ISBN: 978-0-8222-2209-5

★ **THE INTELLIGENT DESIGN OF JENNY CHOW by Rolin Jones.** This irreverent "techno-comedy" chronicles one brilliant woman's quest to determine her heritage and face her fears with the help of her astounding creation called Jenny Chow. "Boldly imagined." *–NY Times.* "Fantastical and funny." *–Variety.* "Harvests many laughs and finally a few tears." *–LA Times.* [3M, 3W] ISBN: 978-0-8222-2071-8

★ **SOUVENIR by Stephen Temperley.** Florence Foster Jenkins, a wealthy society eccentric, suffers under the delusion that she is a great coloratura soprano—when in fact the opposite is true. "Hilarious and deeply touching. Incredibly moving and breathtaking." *–NY Daily News.* "A sweet love letter of a play." *–NY Times.* "Wildly funny. Completely charming." *–Star-Ledger.* [1M, 1W] ISBN: 978-0-8222-2157-9

★ **ICE GLEN by Joan Ackermann.** In this touching period comedy, a beautiful poetess dwells in idyllic obscurity on a Berkshire estate with a band of unlikely cohorts. "A beautifully written story of nature and change." *–Talkin' Broadway.* "A lovely play which will leave you with a lot to think about." *–CurtainUp.* "Funny, moving and witty." *–Metroland (Boston).* [4M, 3W] ISBN: 978-0-8222-2175-3

★ **THE LAST DAYS OF JUDAS ISCARIOT by Stephen Adly Guirgis.** Set in a time-bending, darkly comic world between heaven and hell, this play reexamines the plight and fate of the New Testament's most infamous sinner. "An unforced eloquence that finds the poetry in lowdown street talk." *–NY Times.* "A real jaw-dropper." *–Variety.* "An extraordinary play." *–Guardian (UK).* [10M, 5W] ISBN: 978-0-8222-2082-4

DRAMATISTS PLAY SERVICE, INC.
440 Park Avenue South, New York, NY 10016 212-683-8960 Fax 212-213-1539
postmaster@dramatists.com www.dramatists.com

NEW PLAYS

★ **THE GREAT AMERICAN TRAILER PARK MUSICAL music and lyrics by David Nehls, book by Betsy Kelso.** Pippi, a stripper on the run, has just moved into Armadillo Acres, wreaking havoc among the tenants of Florida's most exclusive trailer park. "Adultery, strippers, murderous ex-boyfriends, Costco and the Ice Capades. Undeniable fun." *–NY Post.* "Joyful and un-ashamedly vulgar." *–The New Yorker.* "Sparkles with treasure." *–New York Sun.* [2M, 5W] ISBN: 978-0-8222-2137-1

★ **MATCH by Stephen Belber.** When a young Seattle couple meet a promi-nent New York choreographer, they are led on a fraught journey that will change their lives forever. "Uproariously funny, deeply moving, enthralling theatre." *–NY Daily News.* "Prolific laughs and ear-to-ear smiles." *–NY Magazine.* [2M, 1W] ISBN: 978-0-8222-2020-6

★ **MR. MARMALADE by Noah Haidle.** Four-year-old Lucy's imaginary friend, Mr. Marmalade, doesn't have much time for her—not to mention he has a cocaine addiction and a penchant for pornography. "Alternately hilarious and heartbreaking." *–The New Yorker.* "A mature and accomplished play." *–LA Times.* "Scathingly observant comedy." *–Miami Herald.* [4M, 2W] ISBN: 978-0-8222-2142-5

★ **MOONLIGHT AND MAGNOLIAS by Ron Hutchinson.** Three men cloister themselves as they work tirelessly to reshape a screenplay that's just not working—*Gone with the Wind.* "Consumers of vintage Hollywood insider stories will eat up Hutchinson's diverting conjecture." *–Variety.* "A lot of fun." *–NY Post.* "A Hollywood dream-factory farce." *–Chicago Sun-Times.* [3M, 1W] ISBN: 978-0-8222-2084-8

★ **THE LEARNED LADIES OF PARK AVENUE by David Grimm, trans-lated and freely adapted from Molière's *Les Femmes Savantes*.** Dicky wants to marry Betty, but her mother's plan is for Betty to wed a most pompous man. "A brave, brainy and barmy revision." *–Hartford Courant.* "A rare but welcome bird in contemporary theatre." *–New Haven Register.* "Roll over Cole Porter." *–Boston Globe.* [5M, 5W] ISBN: 978-0-8222-2135-7

★ **REGRETS ONLY by Paul Rudnick.** A sparkling comedy of Manhattan manners that explores the latest topics in marriage, friendships and squandered riches. "One of the funniest quip-meisters on the planet." *–NY Times.* "Precious moments of hilarity. Devastatingly accurate political and social satire." *–BackStage.* "Great fun." *–CurtainUp.* [3M, 3W] ISBN: 978-0-8222-2223-1

DRAMATISTS PLAY SERVICE, INC.
440 Park Avenue South, New York, NY 10016 212-683-8960 Fax 212-213-1539
postmaster@dramatists.com www.dramatists.com

NEW PLAYS

★ **AFTER ASHLEY by Gina Gionfriddo.** A teenager is unwillingly thrust into the national spotlight when a family tragedy becomes talk-show fodder. "A work that virtually any audience would find accessible." *–NY Times.* "Deft character-ization and caustic humor." *–NY Sun.* "A smart satirical drama." *–Variety.* [4M, 2W] ISBN: 978-0-8222-2099-2

★ **THE RUBY SUNRISE by Rinne Groff.** Twenty-five years after Ruby struggles to realize her dream of inventing the first television, her daughter faces similar battles of faith as she works to get Ruby's story told on network TV. "Measured and intelligent, optimistic yet clear-eyed." *–NY Magazine.* "Maintains an exciting sense of ingenuity." *–Village Voice.* "Sinuous theatrical flair." *–Broadway.com.* [3M, 4W] ISBN: 978-0-8222-2140-1

★ **MY NAME IS RACHEL CORRIE taken from the writings of Rachel Corrie, edited by Alan Rickman and Katharine Viner.** This solo piece tells the story of Rachel Corrie who was killed in Gaza by an Israeli bulldozer set to demol-ish a Palestinian home. "Heartbreaking urgency. An invigoratingly detailed por-trait of a passionate idealist." *–NY Times.* "Deeply authentically human." *–USA Today.* "A stunning dramatization." *–CurtainUp.* [1W] ISBN: 978-0-8222-2222-4

★ **ALMOST, MAINE by John Cariani.** A cast of Mainers (or "Mainiacs" if you prefer) fall in and out of love in ways that only people who live in close proximity to wild moose can do. "A whimsical approach to the joys and perils of romance." *–NY Times.* "Sweet, poignant and witty." *–NY Daily News.* "John Cariani aims for the heart by way of the funny bone." *–Star-Ledger.* [2M, 2W] ISBN: 978-0-8222-2156-2

★ **Mitch Albom's TUESDAYS WITH MORRIE by Jeffrey Hatcher and Mitch Albom, based on the book by Mitch Albom.** The true story of Brandeis University professor Morrie Schwartz and his relationship with his stu-dent Mitch Albom. "A touching, life-affirming, deeply emotional drama." *–NY Daily News.* "You'll laugh. You'll cry." *–Variety.* "Moving and powerful." *–NY Post.* [2M] ISBN: 978-0-8222-2188-3

★ **DOG SEES GOD: CONFESSIONS OF A TEENAGE BLOCKHEAD by Bert V. Royal.** An abused pianist and a pyromaniac ex-girlfriend contribute to the teen-angst of America's most hapless kid. "A welcome antidote to the notion that the *Peanuts* gang provides merely American cuteness." *–NY Times.* "Hysterically funny." *–NY Post.* "The *Peanuts* kids have finally come out of their shells." *–Time Out.* [4M, 4W] ISBN: 978-0-8222-2152-4

DRAMATISTS PLAY SERVICE, INC.
440 Park Avenue South, New York, NY 10016 212-683-8960 Fax 212-213-1539
postmaster@dramatists.com www.dramatists.com

NEW PLAYS

★ **RABBIT HOLE by David Lindsay-Abaire.** Winner of the 2007 Pulitzer Prize. Becca and Howie Corbett have everything a couple could want until a life-shattering accident turns their world upside down. "An intensely emotional examination of grief, laced with wit." –*Variety.* "A transcendent and deeply affecting new play." –*Entertainment Weekly.* "Painstakingly beautiful." –*BackStage.* [2M, 3W] ISBN: 978-0-8222-2154-8

★ **DOUBT, A Parable by John Patrick Shanley.** Winner of the 2005 Pulitzer Prize and Tony Award. Sister Aloysius, a Bronx school principal, takes matters into her own hands when she suspects the young Father Flynn of improper relations with one of the male students. "All the elements come invigoratingly together like clockwork." –*Variety.* "Passionate, exquisite, important, engrossing." –*NY Newsday.* [1M, 3W] ISBN: 978-0-8222-2219-4

★ **THE PILLOWMAN by Martin McDonagh.** In an unnamed totalitarian state, an author of horrific children's stories discovers that someone has been making his stories come true. "A blindingly bright black comedy." –*NY Times.* "McDonagh's least forgiving, bravest play." –*Variety.* "Thoroughly startling and genuinely intimidating." –*Chicago Tribune.* [4M, 5 bit parts (2M, 1W, 1 boy, 1 girl)] ISBN: 978-0-8222-2100-5

★ **GREY GARDENS book by Doug Wright, music by Scott Frankel, lyrics by Michael Korie.** The hilarious and heartbreaking story of Big Edie and Little Edie Bouvier Beale, the eccentric aunt and cousin of Jacqueline Kennedy Onassis, once bright names on the social register who became East Hampton's most notorious recluses. "An experience no passionate theatergoer should miss." –*NY Times.* "A unique and unmissable musical." –*Rolling Stone.* [4M, 3W, 2 girls] ISBN: 978-0-8222-2181-4

★ **THE LITTLE DOG LAUGHED by Douglas Carter Beane.** Mitchell Green could make it big as the hot new leading man in Hollywood if Diane, his agent, could just keep him in the closet. "Devastatingly funny." –*NY Times.* "An out-and-out delight." –*NY Daily News.* "Full of wit and wisdom." –*NY Post.* [2M, 2W] ISBN: 978-0-8222-2226-2

★ **SHINING CITY by Conor McPherson.** A guilt-ridden man reaches out to a therapist after seeing the ghost of his recently deceased wife. "Haunting, inspired and glorious." –*NY Times.* "Simply breathtaking and astonishing." –*Time Out.* "A thoughtful, artful, absorbing new drama." –*Star-Ledger.* [3M, 1W] ISBN: 978-0-8222-2187-6

DRAMATISTS PLAY SERVICE, INC.
440 Park Avenue South, New York, NY 10016   212-683-8960   Fax 212-213-1539
postmaster@dramatists.com   www.dramatists.com